D1259731

CONDEMNED FOR EVER!

CONDEMNED FOR EVER!

WHAT THE BIBLE TEACHES ABOUT ETERNAL PUNISHMENT

Eryl Davies

 EVANGELICAL PRESS

EVANGELICAL PRESS
16/18 High Street, Welwyn, Hertfordshire, AL6 9EQ, England

First published 1987

Unless otherwise indicated, all Scripture references are taken from
the New International Version, Hodder and Stoughton, 1984.

British Library Cataloguing-in-Publication Data:
Davies, Eryl, *1934-*
  condemned for ever! : what the Bible teaches
  about eternal punishment.
  1. Death - Religious aspects -
  Christianity
  I. Title
  248.4   BT825

ISBN 0-85234-241-1

Typeset by Berea Press, Glasgow
Printed in Great Britain by Cox & Wyman, Reading.

To

My parents
for their unselfish care and love.

My wife
who has been my treasured partner for over
twenty-seven years. Her 'price is far above rubies' (Proverbs 31:10).

My children,
Marc and Ann, in the prayer that they, too, will
spend their lives in the service of the Lord Jesus Christ.

Acknowledgements

Without the help and encouragement of my typist, Mrs Elizabeth Pritchard of Anglesey, the publishing of this book would have been delayed indefinitely. For all her work in typing the manuscript, I want to record my deep appreciation.

Due to the pressures of pastoral ministry and then the move recently to theological teaching I was unable to meet the various deadlines agreed with the publisher. However, John Rubens and the directors of Evangelical Press have been most understanding during this pressurized period. I am grateful to them for their support and encouragement.

May God be pleased to bless this book for the conversion and instruction of many, as well as the upholding of 'the faith that was once for all entrusted to the saints' (Jude 3).

To God alone be all the glory.

Eryl Davies
The Evangelical Theological College of Wales
June 1987

Contents

1.
Well, what about it?

Do you remember Diana Dors and her brave fight against abdominal cancer? She was certainly courageous and determined to recover from the surgery she had undergone. And for some months she felt better and free of pain. Diana was confident that she had won her personal fight against cancer and she later appeared on a television documentary series entitled *The Big C*, urging people to face the disease more confidently. The actress, a Roman Catholic, also claimed that God would not let her die of cancer. After two years, however, she again complained of severe stomach pains; she was rushed into hospital in May 1984 and died within a few days. It was a grim reminder to us all of the reality of death. 'Man is destined to die once' (Hebrews 9:27) is the realistic warning of the Bible. Confirming this basic fact, Max Scheler declares, 'It is of the essence of everyone's experience of life, and of our own, that our lives are directed towards death.'[1]

Shortly after Alfred Hitchcock's eightieth birthday in August 1979, Ingrid Bergman visited the famous film director and entertainer in hospital. 'He took both my hands,' she recalls, 'and tears streamed down his face and he said, "Ingrid, I'm going to die," and I said, "But of course you are going to die some time, Hitch – we are all going to die." And then I told him that I, too, had recently been very ill, and that I had thought about it too. And for a moment the logic of that seemed to make him more peaceful.' [2]Ingrid Bergman, of course, was right. We are all going to die, even the rich and famous people. 'The paths of glory', claimed Thomas Gray, 'lead but to the grave', whereas John Dryden affirmed that 'Every man who lives, is born to die,' and he added,

> Like pilgrims to the appointed place we tend:
> The world's an inn, and death the journey's end.

There are some people, however, who try hard to avoid the inevitability of death. In the United States, for example, people pay to have their bodies preserved by deep freezing when they think their own death is imminent. But they do not escape death; they only postpone it, while some actually hasten death by this desperate action.

A South Wales man who dedicated his life to achieving immortality died in January 1986. Mr Gerald Evans founded the controversial Life Extension Society and advocated freezing human bodies for resuscitation later. He argued that when medical science advanced to the stage where they could keep people alive or developed cures for fatal illnesses, the de-iced bodies could be regenerated. The Life Extension Society originally started in the United States and once had a hundred British members but the British branch has since folded.

Others try to escape death by refusing to think about it. They push the disturbing thought to the back of their minds and are too frightened to do anything about it. They are like a person who chooses to ignore the severe pains in his chest and arm, then insists on working rather than consulting a doctor. For some, an accusing conscience and the thought of approaching death are drowned in alcohol or drugs.

Psychologists and sociologists remind us of the fact that people normally die now in a hospital rather than in their own home. For earlier generations a dying person would have been surrounded by his close relatives and neighbours in the intimacy of his home. The entire family, including children, were confronted in this way with the reality of death. There were no drugs, intravenous tubes, oxygen or intricate surgery to relieve the suffering of the dying. Due to the advances in medical science, the situation is very different in our contemporary society. The dying are often transferred to a hospital or hospice where specialized help and facilities are available. For many patients, however, it may be a professional nurse or doctor rather than a relative who stands alongside them in the last moments of life. Perhaps this is one reason why a bereaved person sometimes says, 'You never think it will happen to you!' A few people have foolishly imagined that they will never die. 'No one,' argued Sigmund Freud, 'really believes in his own death.'[3]

Some years ago in a mining valley town in South Wales I met a woman in her mid-sixties who claimed she was never going to die. Her husband had just died and she wanted me to conduct the burial. As we talked inside her small terraced house in front of a large coal fire, she told me she did not intend to die. 'Why not?' I asked in amazement. 'Well,' she replied, 'I have never been ill like my husband and I have always looked after my health. You don't have to

13

die if you don't want to!' Despite my arguments, she remained convinced that death was not for her. Approximately two years after her husband's death, I received a phone-call one morning from a funeral director asking me to conduct the burial of this woman! She had died suddenly during the night after a cardiac arrest. Make no mistake about it: 'Man is destined to die once' (Hebrews 9:27) and 'Death', the Bible claims, 'comes to *all* men, because all sinned' (Romans 5:12).

We are foolish if we deny the fact of death, for the evidence is compelling and frightening. A young man of forty dies from multiple sclerosis after a long, frustrating illness and a businessman dies without warning after a coronary attack. Or it may be the body of a young mother wasting away because of cancer, or a young child dying of leukaemia. Death is no respecter of age, rank or nationality.

The Alamata famine relief centre in Northern Ethiopia was a veritable death camp in 1984. Each day between ninety and a hundred people, mostly children, died as the victims of the greatest and most horrific famine in modern history. Further north at another emergency centre in Koream, some ninety thousand people waited for food and medicine, but the doctor there had supplies for only three thousand. Am I being morbid? No, for death stares us in the face each day in one form or another and some people die in the most dreadful circumstances. Have you realized that, sooner or later, you too must die?

Quite naturally, suffering and death are unwelcome visitors to our lives and families; to lose a close relative is a shattering experience, as Alan Lake found out. On 11 October 1984 the *Daily Mail* carried the front page headline: 'Grieving Husband of Diana Dors Shoots Himself.' In an earlier interview, Alan Lake had said, 'I always thought I'd be the first to go. I knew I could not live without my soulmate. Now that she's gone, I feel completely lost.' Lake felt so lost and sad that he frequently spent hours just sitting and crying beside his wife's grave. One day the grief became so unbearable that after putting their son, Jason, on a train to London for rehearsals with the Royal Shakespeare Company he went home to his £350,000 house in Sunningdale, Berkshire and shot himself.

In God's sight suicide is wrong, for our lives are in God's hand. He alone decides when we die and we must wait God's time. No human has the right to take his own life or the life of another person. Suicide, euthanasia or mercy-killing are not options which we are free to adopt because they are forbidden by God in the Bible. Nevertheless, we can understand the grief and sense of loss felt by Alan Lake for his late wife and his love for her is deeply moving.

There are some philosophers called existentialists who have thought a great deal about death and suicide. The more they thought about death, the more meaningless life appeared to them. For them, 'anxiety', 'dread', 'absurdity' and 'nothingness' were the essential ingredients of human existence. Jean-Paul Sartre, the French novelist born in 1905, was one of these philosophers. Denying the existence of God as well as the genuineness of the Bible, Sartre describes man as a lone individual responsible for choosing his own values and beliefs. Whatever success man achieves or however hard he works, argued Sartre, death hangs over his human existence, mocking him and eventually reducing him and his work to nothing. Overwhelmed by such despair and nothingness, some of these philosophers and others have foolishly chosen suicide as the only solution. But suicide is not the answer to the problems of life and death. It is God alone who gives ultimate meaning and purpose to our human existence; without God and his truth, therefore, we will not be able to understand our lives, as it says in

15

Ecclesiastes 1:2: 'Meaningless! Meaningless! . . . Utterly meaningless! Everything is meaningless.'

There is no need, however, for you to despair like that. Life need not be meaningless, for the living God has given us reliable answers in the Bible concerning all the issues of life and death. The aim of this small book is to summarize in a simple way the teaching of the Bible about death and particularly what happens to unbelievers after death. Are you afraid to die? Do you know where you will go when you die? Is there a real and literal hell? Well, this book will help you to face these questions honestly and practically. Don't stop reading at this point for you owe it to yourself at least to consider the answers which God gives you in the Bible to these questions. Your future depends upon it. Well, what about it? In the next three chapters, we are going to ask three basic questions about death so please read on . . .

1. Quoted by Eberhard Jüngel in *Death: the Riddle and the Mystery*, Westminster Press, Philadelphia, 1974.
2. *The Life of Alfred Hitchcock*, Donald Spoto, Collins, 1983, p.552.
3. *The Complete Psychological Works of Sigmund Freud*, London, 1957, vol.14, p.289.

2.
Why do we have to die?

Human life, of course, would be even more attractive if there were no physical death, for then there would be no funerals, no grieving over loved ones who die, and we should not have to worry about dying ourselves. But as we have seen, physical death is a stark reality. One question we need to ask ourselves then is 'How and why has death entered the world?' Is there an explanation?

Yes, there is a reliable explanation. The Bible tells us that God appointed death for the entire human race. Death is not an accident nor a freak development in the evolutionary process. Not at all; for death was deliberately and justly introduced by God as a punishment on man for his disobedience. Now you will not understand human life nor what is happening in the world unless you grasp this basic point. Think, for example, of the greed, violence, crime and immorality which characterize human life. How do you account for this behaviour? What is the reason for so much unhappiness in the world? Furthermore, why is it that

17

governments cannot agree with each other, fighting and spending vast sums of money on nuclear weapons capable of obliterating all human life on our planet?

If you turn to Genesis chapter 3, in the opening section of the Bible, and to Romans chapter 5, in the New Testament, you will discover how sin and death entered the world. Notice, first of all, what is said in Romans 5, verse 12: 'Sin entered the world through one man . . .' These seven words provide us with a great deal of information. For example, we learn here that sin has not always been in the world. This is a crucial point. In the beginning God created a perfect and harmonious world. There was no wickedness nor sin in the world at that time. When God created the first humans, Adam and Eve, he made them perfect (Genesis 1:27). It is difficult for us to imagine two perfect people – individuals who did not lie, lose their temper, steal nor behave selfishly and cruelly. But that is exactly how God made our first parents. And unlike ourselves, they also knew God intimately and enjoyed obeying him, However, 'Sin entered the world.' In other words, this perfect, happy world created by God was suddenly spoilt when Adam and Eve disobeyed God.

Genesis 3 tells us how sin 'entered the world'. God explicitly commanded Adam and Eve: 'You are free to eat from any tree in the garden; but you must not eat from the tree of the knowledge of good and evil, for when you eat of it you will surely die' (Genesis 2:16-17). Soon afterwards the devil came and lied to them, suggesting that they would not die (v.4) and he encouraged first Eve and then Adam to disobey God's command. The result was disastrous. Both Adam and Eve sinned and in this way sin invaded and affected the entire human race. That was not all. God also punished our first parents, as he had promised. Pain for woman in child-birth, hard work in cultivating the land now cursed with weeds, as well as disease and disharmony, were some of the punishments imposed by God on them and on ourselves (vv.16-19).

There was also more dreadful punishment to come. 'For dust you are,' God told Adam, 'and to dust you will return' and this is the significance of Paul's words in Romans 5:12: 'Sin entered the world through one man, and death by sin . . .' If Adam and Eve had not sinned, neither they nor ourselves would have died; once man had sinned, however, God must carry out his threat of punishment on Adam and the whole human race for 'The wages of sin is death' (Romans 6:23). Perhaps you are appalled at the extent of suffering in the world and feel haunted by the prospect of death. If so, face the facts honestly and don't blame God for the mess the world is in. For it is man, not God, who has spoilt creation and brought all this suffering upon the human race.

Is this fair? After all, you may ask, why should we have to suffer for the disobedience of two people who lived a long time ago? What has it got to do with us in the twentieth century? In order to answer these questions, we must read the remaining part of verse 12 in Romans 5: 'Sin entered the world through one man and death through sin, and in this way death came to all men, because all sinned . . .' Whether we like it or not, the first Adam was the head of the human race and also our representative. An ambassador, for example, represents his government in another country. His job as a representative is to act and speak there as a representative of his country.

Think, however, of a different example. Some fans of Liverpool football club brought discredit to the club and to the whole of Britain by their violent behaviour before the commencement of the European Cup Final in Brussels in May 1985. Forty-two spectators were killed in this shameful incident. Those fans responsible for the violence represented Britain as well as Liverpool. As a result of this violence all English football clubs were banned from playing in other European countries.

Adam, then, was appointed by God as the representative of the entire human race. This was God's decision and as humans we have no right to question the wisdom or rightness of it. Our Creator God chose to deal with the human race as one entity represented by Adam, our first parent. This means that when Adam obeyed we were represented in his obedience, but when he sinned we were all regarded by God as having sinned in Adam, 'And in this way,' insists the apostle Paul, 'death came to all men, because all sinned . . .' Sin, then, entered the world through Adam and physical death is the punishment which God rightly inflicted on Adam and on the human race because of that first act of disobedience.

But the principle of a representative also works to our advantage, because the Lord Jesus Christ became our representative and sin-bearer. An illustration will help to clarify the point for us.

During the Second World War in a Nazi concentration camp a Christian lady explained to a Jewish friend that the Lord Jesus Christ had died on the cross in the place of sinners in order to reconcile them to God. The Jewess, however, was not impressed and failed to see why someone like Christ needed to die in her place. Some weeks later the Jewish lady was standing in a queue of people, waiting, as they mistakenly thought, to go to the washrooms. As she waited in the queue holding her numbered towel over her arm, her Christian friend passed by and realized that the queue was heading for the gas-chambers, not the washrooms. 'Excuse me,' she said to the Jewish lady, 'I have forgotten my soap in the billet. If I hold your towel and keep

your place, would you go and get the soap for me please?'
'Certainly,' replied the friend and off she went several
hundred yards to the billet to get her friend's soap. Five
minutes later she returned to find that the queue had moved
inside and within hours she discovered that her Christian
friend had willingly gone to the gas-chambers and died in
her place, in order that the Jewess could live under another
name and number and eventually leave the camp. This
became a vivid picture to her of the love and sacrifice of the
Lord Jesus Christ, who assumed our human nature in order
to identify himself with us in our need and represent us. As
our representative, he not only obeyed the law which we
have all broken, but he also took our punishment upon
himself and died so that we should live eternally.

After he had preached on the theme of Christ's death one
day, a young girl asked the minister John Elias whether it
was true that Christ died for her sins as well. After giving
her this assurance, John Elias then wrote a hymn based on
the girl's question:

> And was it for my sin
> That Jesus suffered so,
> When moved by his all-powerful love
> He came to earth below?
>
> The holy law fulfilled,
> Atonement now is made,
> And our great debt, too great for us.
> He now has fully paid.
>
> When Jesus bowed his head
> And dying, took our place,
> The veil was rent, a way was found
> To that pure home of grace.

Be thankful then to God for his love in giving us such a glorious representative and substitute as the Lord Jesus Christ, who repairs the damage of sin and death introduced into the human race through Adam. In the next chapter, we shall try to understand what death actually is.

3.
What is death?

'It's obvious,' someone remarks, 'for we all know when a person is dead; if he no longer breathes and his heart stops beating then that person is dead!' Yes, but sometimes the question is much more complex due to major advances in medical science. Problems arise, for example, when a person is kept 'alive' artificially by a 'life-support' machine. Perhaps the patient's brain has been damaged beyond recall yet other organs in the body are maintained by a machine. For example, brain-stem death leads to irreversible coma and medical staff regard this as an adequate criterion of brain death. The patient is then regarded as 'dead' in any meaningful sense of the term, so the 'life-support' machine is withdrawn by doctors. Of course, in most cases death is less controversial and more easily recognized.

What is interesting is that the term 'death' is used in several related but distinct ways in the Bible.

As we should expect, the term frequently refers to *physical* death, in which the union of the body and soul in a human person is temporarily broken. In this context, the Bible often emphasizes the brevity of our physical life in this world. 'What is your life?' asks the apostle James (James 4:14). 'You are a mist [or, a puff of smoke] that appears for a little while and then vanishes.' This is a telling point. A life-span of seventy years, for example, seems a long time, but it is equivalent approximately to only 25,500 days. But if you are now thirty-five years of age, and assuming you reach the age of seventy, you only have about 13,000 days left in which to live here and at least 4,000 or 5,000 of those days you will spend in sleep! This sobering fact of the brevity of our human lives is expressed by Job:

'Man born of woman
  is of few days and full of trouble.
He springs up like a flower and withers away;
  like a fleeting shadow, he does not endure'
                                                    (Job 14:1-2).

It was this fact which filled Pascal, the French mathematician and philosopher, with deep astonishment and fear: 'When I consider the short duration of my life,' he wrote, 'swallowed up in the eternity before and after, the little space which I fill, and even can see, engulfed in the infinite immensity of space of which I am ignorant, and which knows me not, I am astonished being here rather than there, why now rather than then.' [1]

A second use of the term 'death' in the Bible applies to *spiritual* death, that is, the separation of the soul from God which is true of all unbelievers. This is how the apostle Paul uses the term in Ephesians 2:1: 'As for you, you were dead in your transgressions and sins . . .' What a sad picture this is of unbelieving people! As far as seeking God or loving and obeying him are concerned, man is utterly 'dead' and lacks any natural desire or love towards God. In other words, not only are people sinful but sin has radically changed man's moral and spiritual nature. The result of this is that man's mind is blinded to the glorious truths of the gospel, his affections have been diverted from God and from obedience to sinful and worldly things, while man's will is strongly biased against God in favour of self and sin. That is why the Lord said, 'You must be born again' (John 3:7) and insisted that 'No one can come to me unless the Father who sent me draws him' (John 6:44). Unless God radically changes us on the inside by the Holy Spirit we can never become Christians. Our dreadful natural condition, in which we are cut off from God, is described by the Bible as one of spiritual death.

A third use of the term 'death' in the Bible relates to *eternal* death, which is the eternal punishment of unbelievers in hell[2] after death. This is what the Saviour referred to when he told his apostles, 'Do not be afraid of those who kill the body but cannot kill the soul. Rather, be afraid of the One [God] who can destroy both soul and body in hell' (Matthew 10:28). Later we shall examine the Bible's teaching on this important subject so here we shall merely note this further use of the term 'death' in the Scriptures. There is now, however, another question we must ask about death: what happens to us after death?

1. Quoted by W. Barrett in *Irrational Man*, Mercury, London, 1964.
2. Three different words are translated as 'hell' in the Authorized Version of the Bible. The Hebrew word *She'ol* and the Greek *Hades* refer either to the grave or the state of death but also sometimes to the state of the ungodly in hell. The Greek word, *Gehenna* describes the abode and punishment of unbelievers in hell especially after the final judgement.

4.
What happens after death?

Bertrand Russell, the renowned philosopher, is dogmatic in his answer. 'When I die,' he claimed, 'I will no longer exist.' For Russell, a human being is a mere collection of atoms and chemicals which disintegrate at death. During a meal one evening a friend told Russell that she disagreed with his view of death and the afterlife. His reply was brief and unyielding: 'A personality is an aggregate or an organization like a cricket club. I can accept the dissolution of the MCC.' [1] But he was wrong, dreadfully wrong, for man is much more than a collection of atoms. Man was created in the image of God, with a spiritual dimension which continues even after the physical body dies and decomposes, and there are many verses in the Bible which clearly teach the continued and endless existence of both believers and unbelievers beyond the grave. [2]

Many people are less dogmatic than Russell and do not claim to know what happens after death, whereas others believe, however vaguely, in some kind of life after death. In

India and other Eastern countries death is welcomed as a release from the world's evils and as an opportunity afterwards to return in a different form, even as an animal or insect. This theory is called reincarnation. But our main concern in this book is not with what different philosophers, scientists, churches or religions teach, but rather with what God himself says in the Bible. It is not being narrow or prejudiced to do this. For example, would you blame a sick person for ignoring a quack or incompetent doctor and consulting directly with a skilled physician or surgeon? Of course not. In the same way, as dying sinners we require the authoritative word and skilled attention of the living God himself to guide and help us, and it is in the Bible alone that God speaks to us and helps us. Our appeal therefore, will be to the Bible, the Word of God.

In Green's *History of the English People* there is the true story of a missionary who first introduced the gospel to Northumbria approximately 1300 years ago. Paulinus was his name and he was invited to preach in the court of King Edwin of Northumbria. When the missionary arrived in the king's court, he was escorted to a large hall where hundreds of influential people were awaiting him. It was an impressive scene. Courtiers, soldiers and servants all stood around the hall and in the centre sat the king flanked by his guards. Almost immediately Paulinus was introduced to King Edwin and then given permission to address the important audience. He began by affirming that he was an ambassador of a king who ruled the worlds, but as he continued to preach he was suddenly interrupted by an elderly bearded earl. 'Can this new religion', he asked, 'tell us what happens after death? The life of man is like a swallow flying through this lighted hall. It enters in at one door from the darkness outside, and flitting through the light and warmth, passes through the farther door into the dark unknown beyond. Can this new religion solve for us the mystery? What comes to men in the dark, dim unknown?' In reply to the earl, Paulinus repeated the words of the Lord Jesus Christ: 'Do not let your hearts be troubled. Trust in God; trust also in me. In my Father's house are many rooms . . . I am going there to prepare a place for you.' The missionary went on to speak of the gift of everlasting life which God offers to those who believe in Christ.

There certainly is life beyond the grave. This is the clear answer given in the Bible, but this life continues in one of two places, namely, in heaven or in hell.

Heaven

That the soul of the believer goes to heaven at death is the consistent teaching of Scripture. The psalmist says, 'You guide me with your counsel, and afterwards you will take me into glory' (Psalm 73:24). The Lord Jesus himself ascended 'into heaven' (Luke 24:50; Hebrews 9:24) but before his death he prayed, 'Father I want those you have given me to be with me where I am, and to see my glory' (John 17:24). As Stephen was being stoned to death he told his Jewish persecutors, 'Look, I see heaven open and the Son of Man standing at the right hand of God' (Acts 7:56) and his last words were 'Lord Jesus, receive my spirit.' The apostle Paul looked forward to dying in order to 'be with Christ' in heaven, 'which is better by far' (Philippians 1:23). Some years earlier, the same apostle had told the Corinthians, 'We . . . would prefer to be away from the body and at home with the Lord' (2 Corinthians 5:8).

In the seventeenth century, Thomas Brooks, an old Puritan minister, preached a sermon called 'A saint's last day is his best day' [3] based on the opening verse of

Ecclesiastes chapter 7: 'A good name is better than fine perfume, and the day of death better than the day of birth.' During this famous sermon, the minister described death as constituting a major change for the Christian: for example, he exchanges earth for heaven; he exchanges the company of sinful, unbelieving people for that of perfect Christians and angels in heaven; he also exchanges the hard work of praying, fighting sin and resisting the devil for the rest and joys of heaven. 'Blessed are the dead who die in the Lord from now on ... they will rest from their labour ...' (Revelation 14:13).

It is no wonder, therefore, that Billy Bray, the rough Cornish tin-miner converted to Christ early last century, looked forward to going to heaven. As he approached his seventy-fourth birthday in 1868, Billy began to feel extremely weak and ill and he remarked to some friends, 'I think I shall be home to Father's house soon.' His physical condition got steadily worse and a doctor was called to the house. After the doctor examined him, Billy asked, 'Well, doctor, how is it?' 'You are going to die,' was the blunt answer and on hearing these words, Billy Bray immediately shouted, 'Glory! Glory be to God! I shall soon be in heaven.' Then he turned to the doctor and asked, 'When I get up there, shall I give them your compliments, doctor, and tell them you will be coming too?' Just a few hours before he died, a friend asked this old evangelist whether he was afraid to die. 'What?' replied Bray, 'Me fear death? No, my Saviour conquered death!'

Many Christians today look forward to heaven too. On 31 December 1983, for example, a science teacher in North Wales, Gwyn Pritchard, died of cancer at the age of forty-six. Married with three young children, Gwyn was told by doctors for the second time that he had cancer. This time, however, it was incurable. Gwyn's response was a very positive one. 'God has allowed the cancer to appear again for a definite purpose,' he insisted, 'and I have a wonderful God.' He gradually became weaker and more dependent on his wife, Elizabeth, but it was not difficult for Gwyn. God was so real to him that he had a great peace, a peace that everyone noticed and his face would light up as he talked to friends about Jesus Christ. He referred to his sense of honour and privilege at having been placed by God in his illness, for it had been the means of getting to know God more deeply and telling more people about the gospel. On Christmas Day he enjoyed his dinner and then played some games with the children. Gwyn remained in bed after that until he died on New Year's Eve. The day before he died he was again very happy and said he was looking forward to 'going home' to heaven. Before he died he shouted 'Hallelujah!' then chuckled and again said loudly, 'Hallelujah!' If you are a Christian, you are very privileged for you too can look forward to 'an inheritance that can never perish, spoil or fade – kept in heaven for you . . .' (1 Peter 1:4).

Hell

But what about those who are not Christians? Do they go to heaven as well? Listen to the answer given by Jesus Christ: 'Whoever believes in the Son has eternal life, but whoever rejects the Son will not see life, for God's wrath remains on him' (John 3:36). And this, contrary to popular opinion, is the consistent teaching of the Lord Jesus Christ in the Bible. Concluding his famous Sermon on the Mount, Christ refers to two distinct groups of people and two radically different destinies: 'Wide is the gate and broad is the road that leads to destruction, and many enter through it. But small is the gate and narrow the road that leads to life, and only a few find it' (Matthew 7:13-14).

Answering a group of Jews who were curious as to why God had allowed some people to be killed when a building collapsed on top of them, he warned, that 'Unless you repent, you too will all perish' (Luke 13:5). Just a day or two before the Lord was crucified in Jerusalem, he spoke again of the awfulness of judgement for unbelievers, to whom he will say, 'Depart from me, you who are cursed, into the eternal fire prepared for the devil and his angels' (Matthew 25:41). In later chapters, we shall look in detail at many other statements made by Jesus Christ and the apostles concerning the reality of hell, but one thing is clear. The prospect for unbelievers is a dreadful one indeed. There is no hope at all for them if they die without trusting in the Lord Jesus Christ. Whereas, through the grace of God, believers will go to heaven, at death unbelievers will enter hell to suffer justly the eternal punishment of God for their sins. It is this important subject of hell I am going to explain. I want you to know what God says about hell in the Bible. However, I aim to do more than simply convey this information to you. If you are not yet a believer, I want to urge and help you to 'flee from the coming wrath' (Luke 3:7) and to make your peace with God through trusting in the Lord Jesus Christ. What about it?

1. Alan Wood, *The Passionate Sceptic,* Allan & Unwin, 1957, p.236.
2. See, for example, Genesis 1:27; Matthew 10:28; 11:21-24; 12:41; Luke 23:43; John 11:25-27; 2 Corinthians 5:1-10.
3. *Complete Works of Thomas Brooks,* Vol. VI, pp.394-408.

5.
Is it true?

England's worst sporting disaster was on 11 May 1985 when fire destroyed a large, wooden stand in Bradford City football ground. Fifty-three people, mostly pensioners and children, were burned beyond recognition and many more injured in the 1000 degree heat of the fire that destroyed the seventy-seven-year-old stand within four horror-filled minutes. Experienced police officers wept helplessly after huge flames and intense heat halted all rescue attempts; they could only watch people burn to death in their seats.

The Chief Fire Officer for West Yorkshire later revealed that the football club had been warned in a letter six months previously that the stand was a 'fire-trap'. This claim, however, was denied by the club's chairman.

Who was right? Which side should be believed? Within two days the West Yorkshire County Council leader revealed the important letter in a London press conference. He did so, he claimed, 'in the public interest and to avoid further speculation'. There could be no doubt now about the

33

existence of the letter. The claim that the football club had been warned in advance of the fire hazard had been substantiated.

Is your reaction a similar one after thinking about death and hell in the previous chapters? You may feel surprised or shaken to read that there is such a place as hell for unbelievers. Like the football club official, however, you may want to challenge or even deny the facts. To make matters worse, you have heard various people, including bishops, ministers and teachers, deny the existence of hell as well as the virgin birth and resurrection of the Lord Jesus Christ. Perhaps you have accepted their views without thinking seriously about the issue.

The question remains: who is right? Where can I find the truth? Or is it that you are open and reasonably impressed with the evidence so far, yet you still have some nagging doubts and need reassurance, like I did once concerning my examination results?

I was away on holiday in Devon at the time when my examination results were being published. The university was sending the result directly to my home address and a relative had promised to open the official envelope and read the result to me over the telephone. Then, one evening, I was called to the telephone to hear the result. I remember hearing the comforting words: 'Eryl, your name is on the pass-list.' Although I felt relieved, I was not convinced at first. 'Are you sure?' I replied and then asked my relative to check the letter again. Some of the letter's contents were then read to me and I felt much happier about the result. A few days later, however, when I returned home, one of the first things I did was to read and reread the official notification from the university. Only then was I completely reassured that I had passed. It really was true!

Before we go on, therefore, to consider in detail what the Bible teaches about hell, we are pausing to reassure ourselves concerning the Bible. We are referring constantly to the Bible so it is important for us to be satisfied that the Bible is a reliable and truthful book. We can safely build our faith on the teaching of the Bible, for it is the Word of God. The point can be put even more strongly. It is important for us to believe what God says in the Bible rather than accept the fallible, often conflicting, views of friends or even religious leaders. Consider briefly, then, some facts about God and the Bible.

1. God the Revealer

One morning a middle-aged man telephoned me in great need and asked to see me rather urgently that day. I agreed to his request and soon after lunch he was sitting in my study talking about his problems. The man was well-dressed, articulate and kind but agitated and tense. He had clearly suffered a great deal and it was not easy for him to confide in me. I knew nothing about his background or his problems so it was necessary for him to reveal and share with me certain experiences, fears and reactions which had troubled him. As he talked and filled in the details of his problems, I began to understand and respect the man. By the end of our long conversation, I felt I knew him.

Clearly if the man had not first taken the initiative to approach me and then tell me about himself, I would not have known anything at all about him. He would have remained a stranger to me. This kind of situation occurs frequently to all of us and we sometimes feel a sense of surprise when we hear good or bad news from friends or relatives, news we did not anticipate or know beforehand.

Now think of this in relation to God. The word 'reveal' occurs many times in the Bible and its basic meaning is that of unveiling something which is hidden from us and which we could never discover by ourselves. For example, the apostle Paul writes, 'No eye has seen, nor ear has heard, no mind has conceived what God has prepared for those who love him – but God has revealed it to us by his Spirit' (1 Corinthians 2:9-10). In other words, just as that man approached me and told me things about himself, so God has taken the initiative in disclosing his character and purpose to us. Because God has revealed himself to us, it is now possible for us to know a great deal about him and his plans. Now this is a crucial point and one you need to appreciate.

Consider for a moment how great God is. God has no beginning or end and he never changes. He is never ill or tired. Nor will he ever grow old and die. God is also independent. As humans we depend on others for food, work, medicine and education. No one, however, helps God to live or work. He has no need of a teacher or adviser. Just as a very rich bank has no need to borrow money from other sources, so God is complete and infinitely rich in his own being.

Or think of God's greatness in relation to the universe. Almost three-quarters of the earth's surface is under water, an area of approximately 139 million square miles. God it is 'who has measured the waters in the hollow of his hand' (Isaiah 40:12) and determined the boundaries, depth and location of the oceans, rivers and lakes.

But the earth is only one of many planets. Mercury, Venus, Mars, Jupiter, Saturn, Uranus, Neptune and Pluto are some of the more famous planets and there are many more minor planets and asteroids. The earth is 3680 million miles away from the planet Pluto and 93 million miles from

the sun. Referring to this vast expanse of space, the Bible
declares that God 'stretches out the heavens like a canopy,
and spreads them out like a tent to live in' (Isaiah 40:22).
For us the space age only started in October 1957 with the
successful launching of a Russian spacecraft called Sputnik
I, but God created the planets with ease.

'Lift your eyes and look to the heavens:
    Who created all these?
He who brings out the starry host one by one,
    and calls them each by name.
Because of his great power and mighty strength,
    not one of them is missing'   (Isaiah 40:26).

Before this great God, the nations of the earth 'are like
a drop in a bucket' (v.15) and the 'people are like
grasshoppers' (v.22).

As God and Creator, he is apart from the universe,
hidden away from us in unimaginable splendour. While
scientists make exciting discoveries about the universe or
perform intricate transplant surgery, no one can discover
God or his plans apart from his revelation. Zophar asked
Job,

'Can you fathom the mysteries of God,
    Can you probe the limits of the Almighty?
They are higher than the heavens – what can you do?
    They are deeper than the depths of the grave – what
    can you know?
Their measure is longer than the earth
    and wider than the sea'   (Job 11:7-10).

Human reason, then, cannot penetrate the mystery of
God's glorious character and purpose, for he is 'the blessed

37

and only Ruler, the King of kings and Lord of lords, who alone is immortal and who lives in unapproachable light, whom no one has seen or can see' (1 Timothy 6:15-16). His wisdom and knowledge are beyond our grasp too and his ways are beyond tracing out (Romans 11:33). Without God's revelation, we would be helpless to discover anything about him. What is exciting, however, is that God has unveiled himself to us and given us valuable information concerning salvation.

A question may rise in your mind at this point, namely, how has God unveiled himself? Where can we find this information about him? Well, God has revealed himself to us in two basic ways, which we shall now consider briefly.

2. Creation reveals God

As far back as 1854, Sir Alfred Wills, an English judge, became famous for his ascent of the Wetterhorn in the Alps. While this was not the first conquest of the mountain, Sir Alfred's later vivid description of the climb in a book aroused considerable excitement and interest in the climb.

The most difficult part of that climb proved to be the last stage, when the party was hindered by an ice cornice which curved towards them like a tidal wave. This barrier was formidable but the guides hacked away at the cornice for hours until the leading guide could see the blue sky above and, below him, the beautiful valley of Grindelwald. When Sir Alfred Wills made his way through the tunnel and emerged on the summit, he immediately felt he was in the presence of God, who had created the mountain and the majestic scenery around him. Sir Alfred was humbled by the thought of God's power and of his own insignificance in comparison with the glory of God.

Now that is exactly what the Bible teaches. 'The heavens declare the glory of God, the skies proclaim the work of his hands' (Psalm 19:1). In the New Testament the apostle Paul writes, 'For since the creation of the world God's invisible qualities – his eternal power and divine nature – have been clearly seen' (Romans 1:20). In other words, God has stamped his glory upon creation in such a way that when we look at the mountains or seas and open fields, they all testify to the existence, power and eternity of God. In this way, therefore, God has unveiled his greatness in the world around us and 'men are without excuse'. While we can be persuaded of God's existence and power from merely looking at the created world, yet we cannot discover the details of God's character and plans from this general revelation. Nature does not tell us very much about God; what it says is helpful but it is inadequate.

There is another major problem and it is this. God also stamped his law upon our consciences so that men and women everywhere know instinctively what is right and wrong and that God exists. In fact, our consciences often register a protest and make us feel uncomfortably guilty when we break the laws of God. All this again is part of God's general revelation.

But there is a complication. Our own personal sin obscures and deliberately suppresses the revelation of God's greatness in the world around us and also tries to silence the voice of conscience within us. Consequently we are not prepared to acknowledge God even though the evidence stares us in the face. In much the same way that a prejudiced supporter refuses to admit that an opposing team is superior in ability and worthy of winning the game, so men and women by nature are prejudiced by sin against God. We deliberately refuse to admit his greatness or his claims upon our lives.

Once again God has taken the initiative to help us and in the next chapter we shall see how God has revealed himself more fully in the Bible.

6.
God's book

'I wish I had a Bible!' exclaimed a young girl in north-west Wales almost 200 years ago. Her name was Mary Jones. 'The Bible is so important', she decided, 'and I want to know more and more of what God says in this special book.'

You may be familiar with the rest of this fascinating story. Over the following years she learnt to read and, although extremely poor, she saved what little money she could earn in order to buy a Bible. Sometimes Mary went to a nearby farm to read God's Word. Eventually she heard of the Rev. Thomas Charles, in the North Wales town of Bala, who had arranged with people in London for the reprinting of the Welsh Bible. When she had sufficient money her parents allowed Mary, now a teenager, to walk the twenty-five mile journey across desolate, mountainous countryside to the small town of Bala on the shores of Lake Tegid. There she obtained a copy of the Bible but Mary's story left a deep impression on Thomas Charles. He was even more determined now that greater numbers of people should be able to read and own a copy of the Bible. His efforts were greatly rewarded. Not only Wales but many other countries also benefited as he joined with others in founding the British and Foreign Bible Society in 1804, with the specific aim of making Bibles available in many languages.

Although God revealed some aspects of his greatness in his creation, nevertheless he has chosen to give us a more detailed revelation of himself and his plans in the Bible. That is the reason why the Bible is a special book and why people like Mary Jones valued it.

In this chapter and the next we are going to see two important facts about the Bible in order to reassure ourselves that we can safely accept and believe its teaching.

1. The Bible is God's book

The Bible consists of sixty-six individual books, varying in length and written by about forty different writers over a period of 1700 years. For this reason alone the Bible is a remarkable book. The Bible was written originally in Hebrew, Aramaic and Greek on sheets of papyrus, and then copies of parts or, later, the whole of the Bible were handwritten by scribes and even monks over the centuries until the invention of the printing press in the fifteenth century. Throughout this long process, the Bible text has been kept accurate and pure. One confirmation of this was the discovery of the Dead Sea Scrolls in Israel from 1948 onwards. These scrolls were written about 150 B.C. When they are compared with Hebrew Old Testament manuscripts copied around 900 A.D. there is almost complete agreement.

Underlying the whole Bible is an obvious unity and consistency. For example, the Lord Jesus Christ is central in both the Old and New Testaments. He was foretold progressively in the Old Testament; then his coming, life, unique death, resurrection and ascension were recorded and explained in detail for us in the New Testament. Just after his resurrection, the Lord Jesus was walking with two disciples from Jerusalem to the small village of Emmaus, some seven miles away. During that memorable conversation, the Lord 'explained to them what was said in all the Scriptures concerning himself, beginning with Moses and all the Prophets' (Luke 24:27). On another occasion he said, 'These are the Scriptures that testify about me' (John 5:39).

However, it is not just the fact of unity and a central theme which make the Bible so special. There is much more to it. The Bible is unique because it originated with God. He is the real author. Let me explain this.

Writers of individual books, like Moses, David, Jeremiah and others in the Old Testament, and John and Paul, for example, in the New Testament, were not expressing their own view or philosophies when they wrote their books. Nor were they 'inspired' in the sense that Shakespeare was when he wrote his plays, or Beethoven when he composed his symphonies, or Kenny Dalglish when he 'inspired' Liverpool football club to win the league championship and the F.A. Cup in his first season as player-manager. No, the biblical writers did not even have a 'flash' of inspiration or human brilliance. What happened was that God actually 'breathed out' the teaching and the words of Scripture with the result that the prophets and apostles spoke and wrote what God had given: 'All Scripture is God-breathed . . .' (2 Timothy 3:16). In other words, the Bible originates with God, not men.

Phrases like 'the Lord said' and 'the word of the Lord came' appear many times in the Bible. These expressions emphasize that the writers were God's spokesmen, thinking and writing only what God revealed to them. This is true not only of the Gospels but of all the sixty-six books in the Bible.

How did God do this? 2 Peter 1:20 gives us the answer: 'Prophecy never had its origin in the will of man but men spoke from God as they were carried along by the Holy Spirit.' Sometimes with my children I have stood on a small bridge and thrown twigs or leaves into the river below. Quickly we then ran to the other side to see whose twig appeared first from under the bridge. The twigs were certainly 'carried along' by the river. In a similar way when God 'breathed out' his Word, the human writers were 'carried along' and controlled by the Holy Spirit so that they spoke and wrote only what God had revealed.

The Bible is God's book and it is important, therefore, for us to believe what it says, even when it speaks about an unpopular subject like hell.

2. The Bible is God's reliable book

In 1984 a man in Germany was convicted of forging sixty volumes of diaries ascribed to Adolf Hitler. The man, Konrad Kujan, a forty-six-year-old Stuttgart arms dealer, told a Hamburg court that he wrote the first volume in exchange for a uniform once worn by Hitler's Air Force Chief, Marshall Goering. Kujan claimed that he had been prompted to write Hitler's diaries because he had been troubled by the incompleteness of the chronology of that period. The mass circulation magazine *Stern* paid £2.4 million for the diaries which were later proved by an expert to be bogus.

Or think of a different but more serious deception which has misled millions of people for over a century now. The world-wide membership of the Mormon movement is now estimated at over four million people. It was Joseph Smith (1805-1844) who originally founded this movement in the United States. As a teenager he claimed that God had called him to be his special prophet to the world. Some three years later he said that an angel named Moroni disclosed details both of the early history of America and a fuller revelation of the gospel written down supposedly in ancient Egyptian hieroglyphics on gold plates. Smith claimed that these plates were hidden under a hill called Cumorah where they had been since 420 A.D. Exactly four years after the alleged disclosure by Moroni, Smith went to this place and claims to have found the gold plates as well as two crystals which he used to translate the ancient hieroglyphics.

This whole episode was a great fraud. The real story is very different indeed. A Presbyterian preacher by the name of Solomon Spaulding wrote an imaginary history of the primitive Americans called *The Manuscript Found*. No one wanted to publish the script so it was left at a printer's shop in Pittsburgh. The printer named Patterson died within two years and then Rigdon, a frequent caller at the printing shop, found Spaulding's manuscript and used it as a basis for writing *The Book of Mormon* with the help of Joseph Smith and Porley Pratt. Conveniently for them, before anyone else could see them and check Smith's false story, they claimed that the gold plates had disappeared.

What we are interested in is this: can we trust the Bible? Is it a reliable record of God's revelation, or is it some sort of fake like the Hitler diaries or Joseph Smith's book? We do not want to be misled or deceived, especially in such an important matter as hell. For this reason I want to illustrate and confirm the reliability of the Bible and do so briefly in seven related ways in chapters 7 and 8. You need be in no doubt on this point. The Bible really is God's book and, therefore, reliable.

7.
Genuine and trustworthy

Let us now look at some arguments which indicate clearly that the Bible is reliable as the Word of God.

Some characteristics of the Bible

There are several distinctive features about the Bible which mark it out as being a special book.

Think, for example, of the *harmony* in the Bible. There are sixty-six individual books comprising the Bible but, despite the biased claims of critics, particular books or parts of books all confirm and harmonize with the rest of the Bible. As we have already seen, there is also an underlying theme from the beginning to the end of the Bible. That theme is Jesus Christ.

Another feature of the Bible is its *honesty*. The Bible tells us the truth about people. It does not even gloss over the weaknesses and sins of outstanding believers. We are also told uncomplimentary things about ourselves, namely, that we are all sinful by nature and exposed to the anger of God.

The teaching of the Bible is also *profound* and *satisfying*. What is God like? How can we know God? Where have we come from? What is the purpose of our lives? How should we live? Is there life after death? When will the earth end? These are the profound matters which the Bible deals with and answers authoritatively from God.

There is also *power* in the Bible. 'The Word of God is living and active' (Hebrews 4:12). 'I am not ashamed of the gospel,' declared the apostle Paul, 'because it is the power of God for the salvation of everyone who believes' (Romans 1:16). Lives have been dramatically changed, people converted, families blessed, churches instructed and empowered, communities and countries transformed through this wonderful book. As the Word of God, the Bible has tremendous power.

One final feature we shall notice concerning the Bible is its *permanence*. 'The word of the Lord stands for ever' (1 Peter 1:25), despite the hatred of men and their attempts to destroy it.

The famous Voltaire, for example, confidently predicted that Christianity would die during his lifetime and that the Bible would disappear as a book of importance to people. Voltaire was proved wrong. It was Voltaire who died; his Paris home later became the headquarters of the French Bible Society!

Or think of the attempts by the 'Red Guards' in the Chinese Cultural Revolution to destroy both the church and Bibles during the 1960s and 1970s. The loss of Bibles was a tragic loss to the Christians, but the Bible was not destroyed. Far from it. Some Bibles were hidden and saved from the fire. Frequently the believers copied parts of a Bible and Christian radio stations read the Bible at dictation speed for believers with transistors who copied God's Word down in secret. Not only did the Bible survive those difficult years in China; the church also grew enormously. Be sure of this: 'The word of our God stands for ever' (Isaiah 40:8).

The claims of the Bible

There can be no doubt at all that the Bible itself claims to be the Word of God. Time and time again we are told that the Lord spoke to individuals or that the Word of the Lord came to them. What happened was that the Lord put his words on the lips of the prophets and apostles. One such person was Jeremiah.

Around 625 B.C. while he was still a young man, God called Jeremiah to be a prophet. The call was sudden. It was also irresistible. What happened? Jeremiah says, 'The word of the Lord came to me . . .' (Jeremiah 1:4-5). But Jeremiah felt inadequate. He was not an eloquent speaker. Nor did he have any experience in public speaking. Once again the Lord spoke to Jeremiah, reassuring him of his help and presence. Finally the prophet was told by God, 'Now I have put my words in your mouth . . .' (Jeremiah 1:9). Prophets like Jeremiah were conscious of God's words being given to them to speak and write down. They were conscious of the Lord speaking to them and giving them messages from heaven. They were not passing on their own ideas or reflections. Not at all. Their constant claim is that God has revealed the message to them. In the language of the apostle Paul, it means that 'all Scripture is God-breathed' (2 Timothy 3:16).

The character of God

I have a lot of good friends whom I can trust implicitly. They always tell the truth. There is one friend in particular who is scrupulously truthful. I know he would never tell me a lie or try to deceive me. How am I so sure? Well, I know his character well. Now this is even more true in relation to God himself. He is the 'God who does not lie' (Titus 1:2).

On one occasion an unfaithful prophet named Balaam was hired by the pagan King of Moab to pronounce a curse on God's chosen people, Israel. Balaam did his best to please the king and bring defeat upon Israel. However, he failed on three successive occasions because, instead of a curse, God made him utter a blessing upon Israel. On the second occasion when the Moabite king asked Balaam what message the Lord had given him, he replied, 'God is not a man, that he should lie, nor a son of man, that he should change his mind' (Numbers 23:19). God was not only more powerful than Balaam and his witchcraft. He was also truthful and stood by his promises to Israel.

Be assured, therefore, that God will never deceive us in the Bible nor tell us anything in it which is not true. His word through the prophets and apostles can be trusted, for he is a God who cannot lie in any way.

Confirmation from Jesus Christ

Do you still doubt whether the Bible is reliable and divine? Then consider the attitude of the Lord Jesus Christ towards the Old Testament. He is no ordinary or fallible man. Rather he is the Son of God, who is equal with the Father.

The Lord Jesus believed and confirmed many of the historical incidents which are recorded in the Old

Testament. He confirms the creation by God of Adam and Eve (Matthew 19:4). Nor was the story of Jonah being swallowed by a large fish something incredible to the Son of God. Once again he believed and taught this story. In fact he used the incident as a sign of his own death and burial (Matthew 12:42). During the same discourse our Lord refers to the Queen of Sheba's visit to King Solomon in order to hear his exceptional wisdom (Matthew 12:42).

Are you unsure what to make of the stories of Noah and the flood, or Lot and his wife followed by the burning of Sodom? Well, remember that Jesus Christ accepts these stories as real history (Luke 17:26-32). Similarly, he uses the story of Moses and the serpent made out of brass as a real picture of his own death (John 3:14-15).

Many other references could be given but one fact emerges already. This is that Jesus Christ, the Son of God, believed and taught the Old Testament. He regarded it as the Word of God. Indeed he claimed, 'Your word is truth' (John 17:17) and he frequently referred to the words of the Old Testament as settling an issue (Matthew 4:1-10; 19:4-6; 22:29-32). In these respects the Lord Jesus is an example to us. Our attitude to the Bible should be the same as that of our Saviour.

Certain fulfilment

Remember, too, that a great deal of the Bible's teaching and predictions has already been fulfilled. When God says he will do something, he means it and it is certain to take place.

At the very commencement of the world's history, Adam was told not to eat the forbidden fruit of the tree. If he or Eve disobeyed, God threatened that physical death would be introduced as one of the punishments of sin. This happened just as God had warned.

Later, when people again disregarded the Lord, Noah was sent by God to preach repentance to these people. God was very patient and allowed his servant to preach for 120 years before his threat of a world-wide flood was implemented. The people regarded the prospect of a flood as something absurd and impossible. However, they were wrong. Suddenly one day the rains came and within a short time the whole earth was flooded. God had fulfilled his word again.

Abraham was given many promises by God and they were all honoured. One such promise was that he and his wife would have a son. As the years went by, they remained childless. These were frustrating years for this godly couple. Had God forgotten them? Was it too late now? Certainly not. Even at the age of ninety Abraham's wife Sarah conceived and bore a son. Once again God's word had been honoured.

Thus it was for others like Moses, Joshua and David. God's word to them was kept with meticulous care and often these people were amazed at the way in which his promises were fulfilled.

Despite Pharaoh's refusal and opposition, for example, God told Moses that his people would be released from slavery in Egypt. But the situation seemed impossible for Israel. Was God's promise unrealistic? No! Suddenly God put more pressure on the Egyptian king and he was compelled to allow the Israelites to go free from his country. Once again the Lord's word was fulfilled and his people were eventually brought to the promised land, just as God had said. Many times God spoke like this in the Old Testament and each time his word was carried out. His word is reliable.

The greatest promise of all in the Old Testament concerned the coming of the Messiah, the Lord Jesus Christ. Progressively over the centuries this wonderful promise was unveiled by God in greater detail until Isaiah, 700 years before Christ, predicted his virgin birth as well as the glory of his person and work (Isaiah 7:14; 9:6-7; 53:1-12). In God's time, all these prophecies were fulfilled when the Lord Jesus was born at Bethlehem in Judah.

Time and time again the Lord Jesus could say, 'Today this scripture is fulfilled in your hearing' (Luke 4:21). His death, resurrection and ascension to heaven were all in fulfilment of God's word given centuries earlier. Our Lord himself predicted the destruction of Jerusalem in A.D. 70 when nearly a million Jews were massacred by the Romans and the city was completely devastated (Mathew 24:15-28). Should we not also believe the Lord when he speaks about his second coming to the world as judge, or details for us the horrible reality of hell?

Be sure of this: you can trust the Bible. As God's book, many of its prophecies and promises have already been fulfilled. And the same God who warns that hell awaits unbelievers does not speak in vain.

8.
Compelling evidence

Before we return in more detail to the subject of hell in chapter 9, we shall pause to consider two further lines of evidence that the Bible is God's reliable book.

The claims of the apostles

Before his death on the cross, the Lord Jesus gave some important promises to his disciples. One such promise was that 'When . . . the Spirit of truth comes, he will guide you into all truth. He will not speak of his own; he will speak only what he hears, and he will tell you what is yet to come. He will bring glory to me by taking from what is mine and making it known to you. All that belongs to the Father is mine. That is why I said the Spirit will take from what is mine and make it known to you' (John 16:13-15). What the apostles preached and wrote in the New Testament was the truth which the Holy Spirit had revealed to them. The promise of the Lord Jesus had been fulfilled in them. Their words, therefore, were the words of God.

To be an apostle of Christ was a very great privilege. They had been personally chosen by the Lord Jesus. Theirs, too, had been the privilege of accompanying the Lord throughout his three years of ministry. They had heard his teaching, witnessed his miracles and observed him closely. They were also witnesses of his sufferings, death and resurrection. Now, after the Lord's departure for heaven, God spoke through them, thus giving their writings a unique authority.

The apostle Paul emphasizes this in writing to the Galatians: 'I want you to know, brothers, that the gospel I preached is not something that man made up. I did not receive it from any man, nor was I taught it; rather, I received it by revelation from Jesus Christ' (1:11-12). He tells the Corinthian believers the same thing: 'I received from the Lord what I also passed on to you . . .' (1 Corinthians 11:23). In other words, his authority and teaching came directly from the Lord. It is on this foundation of the apostles' teaching that the church of Jesus Christ has been built (Ephesians 2:20-22). Furthermore, this authoritative, apostolic teaching has been recorded reliably in the New Testament for our benefit.

The witness of the Holy Spirit

All the foregoing details concerning the reliability of the Bible have probably stimulated you to think more carefully about the Bible. You may be prepared now to believe that the Bible is the inspired Word of God and, therefore, trustworthy. Certainly the evidence is strong and persuasive.

For the Christian, however, the matter is put beyond all doubt because of the inward witness of the Holy Spirit within him. Think about this briefly.

Before we become Christians, we are prejudiced against God and the Bible. In fact, we cannot understand or appreciate spiritual truth. Our minds are blind to God and his revelation. We even regard the teaching of the Bible as foolish and irrelevant (1 Corinthians 2:14).

When we are born again of the Spirit, our blind eyes are opened to see the greatness of God. We also begin to understand and love the Bible. This is no ordinary book for us now. We begin to revere it as God's Word. What has happened? How did this change of attitude come about? The Bible tells us that a miracle has taken place (John 3:3). That miracle is performed within us by God the Holy Spirit. Our thinking, desires, affections and behaviour are all affected in this glorious miracle. As a result we begin to enjoy reading and hearing the Bible. The Bible has become alive to us. We also have a confidence now that the Bible comes from God and is wholly trustworthy. There is no need of further arguments to persuade us. Now this conviction concerning the Bible has been given to us by the Holy Spirit.

In August 1984 Sotheby's, the London auctioneers, held an auction of items previously belonging to the rock'n'roll group, the Beatles. Altogether the sale raised £207,497. One of the items sold was John Lennon's old school exercise book crammed with his drawings and poems. A staggering £16,000 was paid for it. 'The book was given to me by John Lennon when he left the Liverpool College of Art,' remarked Lennon's friend Rod Murray, 'I've just hung on to it as a bit of the past.' There was no doubt in his mind that the exercise book and its contents had belonged to Lennon. The auctioneers, too, had painstakingly authenticated it as a genuine Lennon possession. Without any doubt, the drawings and poems were the work of Lennon.

As we have now seen, there are compelling reasons why we should accept the Bible as being God's book and completely trustworthy. Prophets and apostles all testify to this. Even the Son of God assures us that the Bible is divine in its origin and reliable in its content. History also illustrates the way in which God's Word has been fulfilled in large measure. To crown all this evidence, the Holy Spirit authenticates for us the divine character and truth of the Bible. We can be more certain that God's book is genuine than Murray and Sotheby's were about Lennon's exercise book.

Now it is this same Bible which talks about hell. Yes, it talks about heaven too. The Bible has a message of hope for the world. We can learn a great deal about God and salvation from the Bible. There is also detailed guidance in its pages as to how we ought to live our lives. But the Bible is honest. It warns us of approaching danger. Facing all unbelievers at death, it warns us, is the awful prospect of eternal punishment. God wants everyone to know of this danger for 'He is patient with you, not wanting anyone to perish, but everyone to come to repentance' (2 Peter 3:9). This gracious God sent his Son on a glorious rescue-mission and this is what the gospel of Christ is all about (John 3:16). The purpose of this book is therefore to alert you to what God says in the Bible about hell. It really is a matter of life and death for you. Believe me, you cannot afford to ignore what the Bible says.

In our next chapter we shall go on to ask another basic question about hell. Is it a real place? We shall, of course, answer the question from God's book. For here alone do we find the right answers to such ultimate and important questions.

9.
Is there a real hell?

Some time ago a group of young people from Great Britain went to an international work camp near Calcutta in India. Their trip was filmed by a BBC T.V. film crew for the *Everyman* series. Needless to say, the young people were appalled at the poverty and suffering they saw in this vast but beautiful country of India populated by 730 million people.

The infant mortality rate in India is high and the average life expectancy for adults is only fifty years. Less than one third of the population have access to clean drinking water and half of Calcutta's population of ten million have no adequate sewerage facilities. Each night almost a million people sleep on the city's pavements or gutters. Tear Fund director George Hoffman remarked that Calcutta 'was the only place in the world where I have seen a decaying human skeleton rotting on a mound of rubbish'. Malcolm Muggeridge has described the city as 'the nearest place to hell on earth'.

We know what Muggeridge means. There are certain conditions and experiences in life which people can only describe in terms of hell. Calcutta is only one example. War is another and more frightening experience.

'Only Hell could compete with the Somme.' That was a national newspaper headline of an article describing the battle of the Somme in 1916. This was one of the most terrible battles ever fought. Some men went to this battle laughing and singing. Many of them were killed. Others were carried away blinded, limbless, with their stomachs shot away and their faces smashed. The British lost 420,000 killed or wounded; the French 194,000 and the Germans 440,000. 'Hell is the only word for it,' remarks ex-soldier Bert Rudd from the Rhondda Valley in South Wales. Another soldier, Ronald Wells, was only seventeen at the time and served in the Machine Gun Corps. 'The shelling, the shooting', he remarked, 'it was hell.'

Perhaps it is the grim ordeal of watching a relative or friend dying that makes you say, 'It was like hell. I never want to go through such a dreadful experience again.'

For others, 'hell' may denote a serious car or air-crash in which a relative died. A terrorist bomb, for example, was responsible for blowing up an Air India jumbo jet in June 1985, killing all 325 people on board. The plane was *en route* from Canada to Bombay. At the time of the explosion the jumbo jet was flying at 31,000 feet and then it suddenly dropped like a bullet into the Atlantic about 120 miles west of Ireland. Dead human bodies were bobbing up and down in the water. Pieces of the wreckage were strewn over a distance of five miles. Only six weeks later 520 people died in a Japanese Airline crash near Tokyo.

For watching relatives and friends, the explosion of the U.S. Space Shuttle *Challenger* in a ball of fire two minutes after lift-off from Cape Canaveral in January 1986 must have been one of the worst moments in their lives. *The Times* newspaper reported the disaster in this way: 'About 75 seconds after launch the shuttle had accelerated to a speed of 1977 m.p.h., three times the speed of sound. It was 10.4 miles up and eight miles out over the ocean. After the explosion, 45 seconds later, one of the *Challenger's* two solid rockets veered to the right and began spiralling through the sky . . . A blazing multi-coloured ball of fire engulfed the shuttle which then seemed to spin out of control, breaking up as it fell.' The crew of seven died instantly in this, the world's worst space flight tragedy.

Or it may be the condition of a person trapped in the fatal world of drugs that merits the description 'hell'. A seventeen-year-old boy addicted to heroin has to scrape £75 a week to buy a finger-nail-sized daily supply of the drug. In an inner-city squat, he lives with other addicts in a filthy room full of blood-stained syringes, burnt remains, empty cans of food, vomit and even human excreta. One friend remarked that the boy was on 'a trip through hell'.

There is no doubt about it. Human life at times can be extremely distressing and painful. Famine conditions, an earthquake or volcanic eruption, war, a crash, terminal illness, drugs, a broken marriage, a violent or sexual attack and injustice all testify eloquently to the harsh realities of life. We appreciate why people want to describe such disasters and experiences in terms of 'hell'. But is this all the word 'hell' means? Many people would flippantly answer in the affirmative. Hell, they claim, only refers to these painful, harsh conditions and experiences in our present lives.

Some go further and argue that you make your own hell on earth. For example, those who flout Bible guidelines concerning sex and marriage are more likely to become infected with the deadly AIDS virus. A government publicity leaflet warns, 'Any man or woman can get the

AIDS virus depending on their behaviour ... There is no cure. And it kills.' A rash decision to marry sometimes results in divorce but only after the wife and children have been battered by the husband. Playing around with soft drugs and glue-sniffing as a child can lead to intolerable suffering and addiction in teenage years. A person who insists on smoking cigarettes is likely to die of lung cancer or thrombosis. The motorist who drives a car immediately after drinking an excessive amount of alcohol may be responsible for killing his passengers as well as other motorists. The resulting sense of guilt can overwhelm and haunt him for a lifetime. What can be worse than this?

These people are obviously reaping the consequences of their foolish behaviour. There is a sense in which they have made their hell on earth. They cannot imagine anything more terrible than what they have gone through in their lives. This is our hell, they tell us, and our hearts go out to them in their anguish and need. However, we must still repeat our question. Is this all the word 'hell' means? Or is there, in addition, a hell beyond this life?

Once again we must turn to the Bible for our answers. Yes, we are responsible for our behaviour and one day we shall be judged by God. Furthermore, 'A man reaps what he sows' (Galatians 6:7). But while we reap some of the consequences of our behaviour in this life, that is not the whole story. The Bible has more to tell us. It leaves us in no doubt that hell is a real place and condition to which unbelievers go after they die. This is what the Bible means when it refers to 'hell'. We shall now note some Bible references which illustrate and confirm this teaching.

The author of Psalm 73 had a problem. Why did God allow the wicked to prosper in the world? Such people prosper (v.3) and seem to have fewer problems than believers (vv.4,5) even though they disregard God. Does it pay to honour God? Is there a reward for the righteous? These are the painful questions the author wrestles with in the first part of the psalm. You may have struggled with these same questions.

However, the psalmist relates how one day he went to worship God in the sanctuary and there, he says, 'I understood their final destiny' (v.17). Those last few words, 'their final destiny', are important. With God's help the writer was able to see beyond the present success and laughter of unbelievers to what will befall them when they die. 'You cast them down to ruin . . .' (v.19) 'Those who are far from you will perish; you destroy all who are unfaithful to you' (v.27). In other words, their hell is not in this life at all but after physical death.

Consider, too, the words of Jesus Christ in the Gospel of Luke, chapter 16, where our Lord relates the story of the rich man and Lazarus. Lazarus was desperately poor and had no choice but to beg for a meagre supply of daily food. Not so the other man; he was rich and lived in the lap of luxury. Eventually both men died and the Lord tells us what happened to them. Lazarus, because he trusted in God, went to heaven (v.22). By contrast, because the rich man was an unbeliever he went immediately to 'hell' when he died. 'In hell' (the Greek word is Hades, which I shall explain later), is how verse 23 begins. This then does not refer to sad experiences or the consequences of foolish behaviour in this life. No, it is rather a place and condition which all unbelievers enter after they die. Our Lord makes it clear that 'hell' is a place of unimaginable suffering and agony for unbelievers (vv.23-28) beyond death.

On another occasion the Lord Jesus urged his disciples: 'Do not be afraid of those who kill the body but cannot kill the soul. Rather, be afraid of the One who can destroy both soul and body in hell' (Matthew 10:28). These last two words, 'in hell', indicate that it is a clearly defined place where unbelievers go.

Furthermore, our Lord also spoke of those who would be 'thrown outside, into the darkness, where there will be weeping and gnashing of teeth' (Matthew 8:12). Unbelievers will hear the awful sentence from the Judge: 'Depart from me, you who are the cursed, into the eternal fire prepared for the devil and his angels' (Matthew 25:41). These are all references to a real place which the Bible calls hell.

Unless we have been rescued personally by Christ, we are all on this road to hell. We are in great danger.

10.
Is it fair?

The likelihood is that you have asked this question on many occasions. Maybe it was when your teacher punished you for something your friend did in class. It was not fair for you to be blamed for someone else's misbehaviour. Perhaps you are a single parent, struggling to re-establish a home for yourself and your young children. You are finding it extremely difficult to cope with all the pressures and the help you need is not forthcoming. It does not seem fair to you.

Or was it fair that over one million Allied and German soldiers were killed in the battle of the Somme in 1916? Historians assure us that this is a pertinent question. In order to relieve the pressure on themselves, the French chose the Somme as the battlefield. The British Commander-in-Chief, Field Marshall Douglas Haig, believed that a powerful artillery barrage would break the German defence line and enable the British infantry to break through. But he was wrong. Winston Churchill disagreed with the choice of the Somme as the battleground and described it as the best-defended position in the world. The German trenches were so well organized and established that they even had pianos to entertain the soldiers. From these trenches they could see for miles over the surrounding slopes and were protected by barbed wire, gun batteries and machine-gun emplacements. Within twenty-four hours the battle had become a disastrous failure. As a result one British general was sent home while another officer at a reunion after the war was insulted publicly by his men. Yes, it seemed so unfair.

But what about the ravages of Africa's famine? More Africans may now die of hunger than the eight and a half million servicemen killed in the First World War. That was the grim warning in 1986 from the director of the UN Office for Emergency Operations in Africa. He claimed that thirty-four million Africans were suffering from severe malnutrition in twenty countries with a total population of 140 million. Is this fair, especially when there is a surplus of food in the West?

Then there was the Chernobyl nuclear plant disaster in April 1986. In addition to the suffering and havoc created in the immediate area of Chernobyl in Russia, other countries have also been seriously affected. For example, a radioactive cloud from the Russian nuclear disaster reached Great Britain. Heavy rains at the time meant a high fall-out of radioactive dust over the country thus increasing the risk of cancer. The National Radiological Protection Board acknowledges that the Chernobyl cloud could cause up to fifty cancer deaths in Britain alone. The radiation can alter radically the chemistry of atoms in living bodies. One cannot help asking, is it fair that so many ordinary people are affected adversely by the world's worst nuclear accident at Chernobyl or even by other nuclear accidents?

In much the same way people respond to the Bible's teaching about hell. 'It's not fair,' they insist. 'What have we done to deserve such suffering? Anyway, I thought he was a loving God. Surely he will not send people to hell. No, it would not be fair.'

Is this your reaction? Are you unable to reconcile the love of God with his punishment of unbelievers in hell? If so, I invite you to look at all of the facts. You may have collected a few pieces of the jigsaw, but you need other pieces as well before you will be able to see the full picture.

Most of the additional pieces you need concern God himself and without these vital pieces you will never be able to fit the jigsaw together. We have a problem here too. Our thinking is instinctively man-centred and biased against God. Now this is reflected when we consider a subject like hell. For example, we do not approach the subject from God's standpoint and, consequently, it does not seem fair to us that God should punish sinners. But there are three important pieces of the jigsaw you need before you can appreciate the full, biblical picture of hell. These are God's greatness, God's holiness and, finally, God's anger. We shall begin by considering God's greatness.

God's greatness

It was an unforgettable evening. At the time I was a first-year university student and sharing lodgings with five other students, one of whom was a final-year economics student from Uganda, who was also the president of the university debating society. On this particular evening, it was his responsibility to meet and look after the distinguished guest-speaker before the society's annual meeting. The guest-speaker was the former post-war Labour prime minister,

Clement Attlee. My friend met his important guest at the railway station and took him immediately to a hotel for a meal. Then, on his way to the debating society, my Ugandan friend brought Clement Attlee to our lodgings to meet us. I remember it well. Clement Attlee was a small, bespectacled man but by this time old and frail. We shook hands and talked briefly with him and felt a deep sense of honour in having met such a great man.

On a different occasion, I was to receive a post-graduate degree from the Queen Mother at the Royal Albert Hall in London. The scene was impressive and majestic. All the graduating students were attractively dressed, with their appropriate cap, gown and hood. Relatives, friends and administrators filled the vast hall. A military band was in attendance too. At 2.30 p.m. precisely, there was a fanfare of trumpets heralding the procession of university professors, officials and city dignitaries into the hall. The congregation stood and the people eagerly waited to catch a glimpse of the Queen Mother. Towards the rear, there she was, dressed in her colourful gown as University Chancellor. Nearly two hours later, it was my privilege to be introduced on stage to the Queen Mother and to shake hands with her. That again was a memorable occasion.

In a much deeper way this was how Isaiah the prophet felt when he 'saw' God in the temple. To Isaiah, God was infinitely great. When he 'saw the Lord' (the Hebrew word here is *Adonai*) he saw one who is great and able to carry out all his plans (Isaiah 6:1). He is no weakling. There is no failure with God. 'My purpose will stand,' he declares, 'and I will do all that I please' (Isaiah 46:10). The plans of a young person for a career may never materialize, possibly due to examination failure, keen competition or ill health. We are all aware of a basic inability to carry out plans which are so important to us. God, however, never fails. He planned to bring the Jews out of slavery in Egypt but Pharaoh was unwilling. Did God have to abandon or modify his plan? No. God's plan was carried out perfectly. Despite the rage and malice of men, the evil and ceaseless attacks of Satan and even the weaknesses of believers, the Lord will carry out his plans.

But Isaiah also saw the Lord 'seated on a throne' as the sovereign Ruler of the universe. Can God really be in control of this sad and violent world? The Bible says 'Yes'. God 'works out everything in conformity with the purpose of his will . . .' (Ephesians 1:11). The winds, seas, rain, sun, moon, stars, all living creatures, men, angels and demons are all governed by God. The wicked as well as the believing are subject to his rule. 'The Lord reigns' (Psalm 97:1). There is no one higher or greater than God. No one can rival him. 'Yours, O Lord, is the greatness and the power and the glory and the majesty and the splendour . . . You are exalted as head over all' (1 Chronicles 29:11). People cannot force God to do anything. God alone freely decides what he will do, what and whom he will create and the details and destiny of our lives. 'Our God is in heaven; he does whatever pleases him' (Psalm 115:3). He is the supreme King.

Isaiah also saw the Lord as being 'high and exalted'. In other words, he is apart from us, separate, independent and glorious. He is not a mere superman. Rather he is 'the high and lofty One who inhabits eternity' (Isaiah 57:15, AV). The beauty and majesty of his person are incomparable and certainly overwhelming for humans and even angels. Isaiah was compelled to cry out, 'Woe to me! I am ruined! For I am a man of unclean lips . . . and my eyes have seen the King, the Lord Almighty' (Isaiah 6:5).

Now if you consider properly this piece of the jigsaw, you will conclude that God is fair to punish sinners in hell. You see, it is in relation to God that sin assumes its essential significance; sin is not a mere defect or weakness in man or an unsociable action but rather an offence against God. 'Against you, you only, have I sinned and done what is evil in your sight,' confessed David after his sin of adultery (Psalm 51:4). When Joseph was approached by a married woman and encouraged to go to bed with her, he refused, exclaiming, 'How then could I do such a wicked thing and sin against God?' (Genesis 39:9)

Sin, then, is rebellion against God. Just as a child can rebel against its parents, or citizens rebel against the laws of a country, so sin is active rebellion on our part against God. We rebel, however, because we are opposed to God and his commands; we prefer to go our own way. Sin is an insult to God and an affront to his authority. The evil of sin is that it is committed against this great God who deserves and demands to be obeyed.

There is no doubt about it. It was a privilege to meet, albeit briefly, a former prime minister and the Queen Mother. I felt overawed by them. Certainly I would not have wanted to insult them or disregard their wishes. God, however, is infinitely greater than any earthly ruler, yet we are prepared to offend him and disobey his commands. Once you begin to see God's greatness you will never doubt the fact that sinners deserve to be punished by God in hell.

11.
It is fair

We are still fitting together the final pieces of the jigsaw. One important piece, namely God's greatness, was put into place in the previous chapter. Now we are going to consider two other pieces, God's holiness and anger, which will complete our picture and demonstrate the fairness of hell.

God's holiness

The year was 740 B.C. Feeling discouraged and fearful for his nation's future, a young statesman made his way to the temple in Jerusalem to worship God. His name was Isaiah. While he worshipped, Isaiah was given a glorious vision of God and then called to be a prophet.

Isaiah saw God, first of all, as a great king sitting on his throne. He witnessed a breath-taking scene of great majesty and glory as the seraphim in heaven worshipped God. As an expression of reverence before the holy God, each seraph

71

covered its face with two wings, for they could not look directly on God. Around the throne of heaven the seraphim shouted God's praise, declaring, 'Holy, holy, holy is the Lord Almighty; the whole earth is full of his glory' (Isaiah 6:3). Gripped by this sight of the holiness of God, Isaiah felt condemned as he acknowledged his sinfulness before such a great God. Isaiah knew that he deserved to be punished by this holy God.

But what does it mean to say that God is holy? How can we understand this description? Well, the Bible says three things at least about the holiness of God.

First of all, *God is holy in his nature.* A man can pull his coat or jacket off, but God cannot pull his holiness off. The reason is that holiness is not something God wears or does, but it is his nature. As such, holiness is inseparable from God.

This means that God does not have to decide to be holy. You may decide to improve your life. Perhaps you are ashamed of the lies you have told or the selfish behaviour which has affected other people. There are bad habits, too, which you feel you want to be rid of. You have, therefore, turned over a new leaf and decided to live differently. By contrast, God never has to decide to be different or better, for he is always holy. That is his nature and it is impossible for him to be otherwise. Even at Calvary God did not stop being holy for there he punished his own beloved Son, the Lord Jesus, as a substitute for our sin. Remember then that God's nature is holy.

Secondly, holiness means that *God is free of all sin.* We are so accustomed to seeing sin in our own lives and in the lives of people around us that it is extremely difficult even to imagine a person like God, who never sins. Certainly sin stares us in the face all the time. Violence, hatred, adultery, rape, robbery, murder, dishonesty and lying are only a few of the sins we hear about daily on the T.V. If you are honest, you can see a lot that is wrong with your own life. Perhaps you would be too ashamed to share some of your secret thoughts with your closest relative or friend. The Bible indeed is right: 'All have sinned and fall short of the glory of God' (Romans 3:23). By contrast, God never sins. There is no trace of evil or imperfection in God. 'God is light; and in him there is no darkness at all' (1 John 1:5). Because God is holy, it is impossible for him to sin.

Thirdly, God's holiness means that *he hates sin with an intense hatred*. Let me illustrate the point in several ways. At present many people throughout the world are appalled at the policy of apartheid in South Africa, a policy in which black people are segregated from white people and treated in an inferior way. Some governments have applied economic sanctions to South Africa as an expression of their hatred of apartheid and their determination to abolish the policy.

Or come with me outside an English law court. A man has just been charged with the murder and rape of a young girl and he is being escorted by the police from the court to a waiting car which will take him to prison. When the charged man steps outside the court, the angry crowd surges forward shouting and jeering at him. Some even try to run up to the prisoner and hit him but are prevented by the police. The people obviously hate the man and his evil crimes.

Nevertheless, however strong the reactions of people may be towards certain crimes or forms of injustice, unbelievers are themselves inconsistent in their hatred towards sin. For example, a man may hate apartheid in South Africa and yet be a racist in his own country. Similarly a husband may deplore the callousness of the rapist but himself be guilty of beating his own wife or committing adultery. Or maybe it is an employee who campaigns against corruption in his union or in local government, yet secretly steals from his employer or lies to the tax authorities about his personal income. There are glaring inconsistencies which reveal that the hatred of unbelievers towards sin is only partial.

For the Christian, on the other hand, it is different, although he or she is far from being perfect. Having been changed inwardly and powerfully by the Holy Spirit in the new birth (John 3:3-7), the believer hates everything which violates the holy law of God (e.g. Exodus 32:19; Acts 17:16). Yes, he hates his own secret sins and tries to turn from them in obedience to God. He also hates the sins he sees in society, which at times make him feel sick as well as sad.

But have you ever realized that God also hates sin? In fact, his hatred of sin is intense and perfect. Quite literally, God cannot stand sin. All sin is offensive to God.

> 'You are not a God who takes pleasure in evil,
>   with you the wicked cannot dwell.
> The arrogant cannot stand in your presence,
>   you hate all who do wrong.
> You destroy those who tell lies,
>   bloodthirsty and deceitful men
>   the Lord abhors'   (Psalm 5:4-6).

The hatred of sin which believers, or even angels in heaven, possess cannot be compared with God's hatred of sin. It is only like the feeble light of a matchstick on a dark country road compared with the blaze and light of the sun at midday. Such is the contrast. It is because God hates sin that he punishes sinners in hell. When you understand God's holiness, you have no choice but to acknowledge that it is fair for sinners to go to hell.

Now we turn to consider the final piece in the jigsaw, namely, the anger of God.

God's anger

Get this clear from the outset: anger in God does not mean he is irritable, bad-tempered or unpredictable in his reactions. Far from it. In fact, anger or wrath is an essential quality belonging to the character of God. As such, anger describes the controlled and permanent opposition of God's holy nature to all sin. Such opposition to sin on God's part is not a whim or a mere decision or occasional mood, but the reaction of his perfect holy nature to sin. Anger, then, is as essential to the nature of God as is love; without anger God would not be God.

Furthermore, the Bible makes it clear that this anger is not something God keeps to himself and hides from people. Rather it is an anger God is continually revealing towards sinners (Romans 1:18).

To convince you of this point, I want to remind you of some obvious expressions of God's anger in Bible history. Only Noah and his small family took any notice of God and his Word in the early history of the human race. Although God sent Noah to preach repentance to the people, they were not interested at all in God. They were having a good time, or so they thought. Life was busy and exciting for them. Patiently God waited. He waited for over a hundred years. Eventually God ordered Noah to take his family into the ark. The reason? God was going to flood the world in his anger and destroy the rest of the human race. His threats were not idle threats at all. God really is angry against sin and you can read about this history in Genesis chapters 6-9.

Some time later God was angry with the cities of Sodom and Gomorrah. Why? Well, the people living there were unbelievers and they disobeyed God. For these reasons alone they were exposed to the anger of God. But there was more to it. They also practised some of the most base and immoral sins possible and so God destroyed those cities by fire (Genesis chapters 18-19).

Not even God's chosen people, Israel, escaped this anger of God. Whether in the wilderness or in the period of the judges or prior to the exile in Babylon, God's anger was regularly aroused into action against their sin and unbelief. The destruction of both the temple and Jerusalem in 586 B.C. and again, but more devastatingly, in A.D. 70, were expressions of God's wrath on the nation of Israel.

There are other ways, too, in which God's anger is expressed, but at this point I want you to observe how this anger of God falls finally and irrevocably on unbelievers, thus making hell an awful reality.

While unbelievers go immediately to hell at death (see Hebrews 9:27; Luke 16:22-28), the Bible also teaches that the anger of God will reach its climax and burst in like a flood upon unbelievers when the Lord Jesus Christ returns in glory to judge the world.

Some years ago I climbed Cader Idris mountain near Dolgellau in North Wales with a group of young people. It was a beautiful, warm day with blue skies and a gentle breeze. Before starting the climb, I enquired whether I needed to take my plastic raincoat with me. 'No,' was the firm reply from the leader, 'it's a lovely day and it won't rain today.' Foolishly, I heeded his advice. We climbed slowly, enjoying the beautiful scenery, then stopping to talk and drink at regular intervals. As we eventually neared the summit, we noticed some dark, low clouds coming rather quickly towards us. Within minutes, we were enveloped by the clouds. There was a gentle shower of rain at first with the threat of more to come. We knew there was no time to waste. As we started to walk quickly down the mountain the showers of rain became heavier, restricting our vision and making the ground under our feet slippery and dangerous.

Yes, we were wet, very wet indeed. What had begun as only a slight drizzle of rain had by now developed into a heavy downpour. It seemed as if the heavens had released all their water upon us.

Something like this is going to happen at the end of the world when the Lord Jesus Christ returns. There have been showers of divine anger falling upon people continually since the time of Adam and Eve. These showers, though unpleasant to people, have been light or moderate and have fallen on individuals or groups of people who rebelled against God. They deserve to be dealt with by God in this way. The Bible teaches, however, that these light or moderate showers of divine anger will one day become a cloudburst falling on all unbelievers in the world. This will be the final 'day of wrath and revelation of the righteous judgement of God' (Romans 2:5, AV). It was this final downpour of God's anger which John the Baptist referred to when he challenged a group of religious leaders, 'Who warned you to flee from the coming wrath?' (Matthew 3:7) Some of our Lord's parables also stress this point, as, for example, in the imagery of the final 'harvest' at the end of the world (Matthew 13:24-30,36-43).

Be under no illusion. Unbelievers deserve to go to hell. And it is fair for God to send them there. Don't blame God or say it is unfair. Man it is who has sinned. He is the rebel who continues to defy God and break his holy laws. In his heart he hates God and refuses to honour or serve him. He does not want God to interfere with his life or tell him how to live. And man is without excuse. The evidence stares him in the face. Even creation tells him that God exists and that God is powerful as well as eternal. Man's conscience also tells him of his duty to obey God. There is the Bible, too, which reveals God to man. But man ignores the evidence. He continues to sin without realizing that God, in his holiness and anger, must punish him for his disobedience. 'The soul who sins is the one who will die' (Ezekiel 18:4).

A young man in Germany in 1505 had just obtained his M.A. degree and had commenced further studies in law. In spite of his university attainments, he was depressed. He himself tells us why. His sin troubled him and he was frightened of dying for then he would have to meet God as Judge. Martin Luther knew that God was holy and also angry towards sinners. His heart sank at the prospect of death for he knew that he deserved to go to hell. But how could he be right with God and win favour with him? How could he avoid going to hell? That was his big problem.

After only half a term studying law, Luther returned home for a brief holiday. On his return to college, he was walking along a lonely country road when a dreadful storm broke out. The young man was frightened, especially after lightning threw him to the ground. He prayed in fear. Such was his fear that he vowed he would become a monk if God spared his life. His life was spared and, within a few days, he kept his promise and entered a monastery. Now he began a more earnest search for God and salvation.

After some months in the monastery Luther realized he had failed to satisfy God at every point despite a strict and religious life. 'I was a good monk,' he remarked, 'and I kept the rules of the order so strictly that I may say that if ever a monk got to heaven by his monkery, it was I. If I had kept on any longer, I should have killed myself with vigils, fastings, prayers and readings.' His spiritual problem was eventually solved through the Bible as God showed him that Jesus Christ alone had kept the law of God on our behalf and fully suffered the punishment for sinners when he died on the cross. At last, he found peace with God through trusting in Christ. He knew now that his sins were all forgiven through the Lord Jesus Christ.

No, not even Luther deserved to be forgiven by God and he would have been the first to admit this. He was a sinner like ourselves. However, God is wonderfully kind and merciful towards us all. He offers a free pardon and salvation to hell-deserving sinners because 'Christ died for sins once for all, the righteous for the unrighteous, to bring you to God' (1 Peter 3:18).

Accept God's salvation now before the cloud of his anger falls upon you for ever.

12.
Is it really so awful?

Well, it depends, of course, what you are referring to. Are you anxiously waiting for your examination results? Perhaps you are desperately worried in case you fail. There is also the worry of how you or your family will cope with the disappointment. You cannot help asking yourself the question: is it really so awful failing an examination?

Or it may be you are unemployed and the prospects of another job are bleak. You always feared being made redundant or hearing that your firm had collapsed. Now it has happened. Somehow you have now lost your sense of dignity by not being able to earn a wage and support your family. Depression has set in and life seems to have less meaning. For you, being unemployed is an awful, harrowing experience.

But your problem may be very different. You have not lost your job or failed an examination. In a sense, your problem is much worse. Your life is threatened by disease. Treatment is needed and there is no time to waste. Panic gripped you when the doctor gave you the diagnosis. This is the most awful moment in your life.

Our question, however, can also be asked in relation to less personal but equally important matters.

The mystery of a massive hole in the ozone layer is one such matter. The ozone layer filters the cancer-causing ultra-violet rays from the sun. Scientists now fear that man-made pollution from spray cans and gases has caused the hole which appears each September and October and which has dramatically expanded to the size of the United States. 'It could be the leading edge of something more detrimental,' a NASA scientist remarked recently at the Goddard Space Flight Centre. 'It could expand outwards to more populated areas. We just don't know right now,' he added.

The ozone is so thin over Antartica when the hole appears that ultra-violet radiation produces a tan even in the pale October sun. These same conditions in a populated area would cause a sharp increase in skin cancer and also wipe out plankton and fish larvae and kill aquatic life, as well as reducing crop harvests rather drastically. It really could make life on earth quite awful for us.

Many people are worried about the possibility of a nuclear war which could obliterate all human life and ravage the earth too. Pierre Berchlet, a French scientist, wrote these remarkable words in 1860: 'I believe that inside 100 years of physical and chemical science, man will know what the atom is.' He was right. In fact, with fifteen years to spare his prediction about the atom was fulfilled when the United States used the atom bomb for the first time over Japan in 1945. Berchlet added, 'When science has reached that stage, it will soon be time for God to come down to earth with his bunch of big keys and say to the human race, "It is closing-up time." '

Consider Hiroshima for a moment. The atom bomb seared to death all animals and humans in the city. Those who were outside when the bomb exploded were burned to death while those indoors were killed by the indescribable pressure of the heat. Over 70,000 people in Hiroshima were killed immediately and so intense was the heat that it was impossible to distinguish men from women among the dead. During the following months and even years, large numbers of people suffered and died as a direct result of the atom bomb – an awful, awful incident indeed!

A nuclear war, however, will be much worse than anything experienced in Hiroshima. An American Government spokesman has estimated that in a nuclear war between NATO and the Warsaw Pact about 160 million Americans would die almost immediately and the same number of Russians. The total population of Western Europe would be destroyed in such a war. Even more awful would be 'star-wars' in which manned satellites in space loaded with chemicals and bombs would be poised to destroy not only cities but countries and continents. Such things, of course, may never happen but if they do, the suffering and devastation will be terrible indeed.

But what about hell? Are we making an unnecessary fuss about it? Is hell as awful as the Bible suggests? These are fair questions and they demand honest answers.

Once again we have to turn to the Bible for these answers. However, I must warn you that the Bible pulls no punches; it says that hell is an awful place and infinitely more dreadful than a Hiroshima or a nuclear war.

Why is hell so awful? What does it involve? How will unbelievers suffer there? In order to answer these and other questions, we shall group together, and comment briefly on, some of the descriptions of hell given in the Bible but we shall do so under two main headings: first, separation and, in the next chapter, punishment. These two factors of separation and punishment make hell a most dreadful place.

Separation

We know only too well what separation means in everyday life. Sometimes there is what we call an involuntary separation. A young courting couple who live miles apart are separated unwillingly for days or weeks at a time and it is painful for them. There are occasions, too, when a husband has to be away on business for long periods but both partners long to be together again. More unwelcome still is the death of a marriage partner. This is an involuntary separation in the sense that neither partner would have chosen death. The couple loved each other and longed to be together. They fought the disease and did all they could to halt the approach of death, but it was all in vain.

There can also be voluntary separations. Because of ageing parents or other domestic pressures a couple may lovingly and willingly agree to release a partner for days on end in order to nurse or assist a relative. Sadly a couple may discover that they are unsuited to each other and agree amicably to separate. Or it may be a sports star who agrees voluntarily with a club to move elsewhere.

Sometimes it is necessary to have a more legal, enforced separation or divorce, as, for example, when a couple go to court to legalize their separation. If the husband has threatened and battered his wife on numerous occasions the court may stipulate that he must not go near her any more. Or, in an attempt to curb violence, certain hooligans who have behaved violently in football matches have been banned by courts from attending matches in the future.

While examples of separation in human life can be multiplied, I want to remind you that one essential feature of hell is separation, that is, separation from the love and kindness of God.

Our Lord described hell in this way on at least two occasions. The first was in his famous Sermon on the Mount where in the concluding section he describes unbelievers at the last day pleading for admission to heaven. Some of the people had been involved in dramatic miracles, exorcisms and prophecies. They believed in healing and had seen the power of God at work in other people's lives. The tragedy was that they themselves had never been converted. They were nominal believers but their hearts had not been changed by the Holy Spirit and there was no obedience in their lives to the holy law of God. It is to these people that the Lord Jesus says, 'I never knew you. Away from me . . . ' (Matthew 7:23).

On the second occasion, the Lord pictures himself judging all the peoples of the world at the final judgement. Once again he tells the unbelievers, 'Depart from me, you who are cursed, into the eternal fire prepared for the devil and his angels' (Matthew 25:41).

'So what?' you may be asking. 'I don't care if he says that to me. I'll manage all right without Christ even after I die.' But will you? Ponder the matter carefully and notice the significance of the word 'depart' which our Lord uses.

To 'depart' means that Christ, the Judge, rejects you. He refuses to allow you into heaven. The door is shut in your face. In this way, you are removed from his mercy and help. If this happens to you, your plight will be a terrible one indeed. But how terrible?

Well, first of all, you will be separated as an unbeliever from the kindness and goodness of God. Perhaps you have never appreciated this before so I invite you to consider it

85

for a moment. The most important work going on in the world is the salvation of a vast number of sinners from different backgrounds and countries. God chose them before the world was created (Ephesians 1:4) and it is for their sins that Christ died (Ephesians 5:25-27; 2 Corinthians 5:21). In God's appointed time, the Holy Spirit is sent to bring these sinners individually to faith in the Lord Jesus Christ (John 6:44; 1 Corinthians 2:9-14). These believers are then indwelt and helped by the Holy Spirit (1 Corinthians 3:16; Ephesians 2:22). They are also provided for materially by God and protected in this world (Psalm 34:10; 1 Kings 17:1-6; Romans 8:31-39; 1 Peter 1:5). In other words, Christians are a very privileged people indeed.

Now when God sends his sun to shine on believers, he does not confine the sunshine to the houses, streets or even countries where they are living. Nor does he confine the rain to the gardens or reservoirs of believers (Matthew 5:45). To give security, care and preparation for an integrated life in society, God has wisely put individuals in families (Psalm 68:6). In this way he especially cares for believers but he generously allows unbelievers to enjoy this stable provision. There are experiences, too, in which both groups can find enjoyment and fulfilment in God-given relationships and responsibilities. It is God who appoints governments and magistrates to govern us in order to encourage the law-abiding and punish the lawbreakers.

During the last World War, my father worked on the railway and sometimes he would be responsible for moving troops from one part of the country to the other. When he was moving American troops he would return home with a bag full of chocolates, sweets, wrapped cream biscuits and chewing-gum, the like of which we had not seen before because of severe rationing conditions. My father, of course, was not an American nor was he a soldier, but as he travelled with the American troops he benefited greatly from their presence in Britain.

This is a picture of God's dealing with the world. Unbelievers are not part of the glorious church of Jesus Christ yet they benefit greatly from the presence of the church in the world and God's love towards it. In hell, however, unbelievers will be deprived of all these benefits and they will be separated from the kindness and goodness of God. That in itself will be dreadful.

But there is more. In hell you will be cut off from God's mercy and salvation. As this bare statement may not mean very much to you, I want to illustrate the importance of Christ's sacrifice for sinners.

Imagine a boy who falls into a dangerous river where there is a fast-moving current. The boy is a poor swimmer and unable to cope with the current. There seems no doubt that he is going to drown. However, a man who is walking along the river-bank sees the danger the boy is in and he acts immediately. He pulls off his jacket and shoes, then dives into the river to rescue the boy. Even the strong man experiences difficulties but he eventually reaches the drowning boy. Holding the frightened child tightly, he quickly turns around and swims slowly back to the river-bank. Within yards of the firm, dry ground, the swimmer finds himself in trouble. The current suddenly becomes too strong and pulls him away. There is no time to be lost. He pushes the boy to safety but within seconds the swimmer is caught in a vicious whirlpool and drowned.

Now this is a picture of what the Lord Jesus Christ did for us. As humans, we are all like that drowning boy. No, of course, we are not drowning in a river. Our predicament is far worse. We are drowning in the river of our sins and the tide of God's anger will soon sweep us away to hell. And, despite our efforts, we cannot save ourselves. There seems no hope at all for us. But listen, God has taken the initiative to help us. He sent his only-begotten Son into the world on a glorious but costly rescue mission. In order to save us from drowning in the swelling tide of God's wrath, Christ took our place on the cross where 'the Lord has laid on him the iniquity of us all' (Isaiah 53:6). It was costly indeed, for Jesus Christ 'poured out his life unto death' and 'was numbered with the transgressors. For he bore the sin of many . . .' (v.12).

This same Lord Jesus Christ is still able and willing to save sinners. In fact, he invites you to trust him and receive his great salvation (e.g. Matthew 11:28-30; John 1:12-13; 7:37, etc). All you must do is to believe (Ephesians 2:8-9). But be warned: if you die without having being rescued by the Saviour, you will hear those dreadful words: 'Depart from me . . .' Whatever your arguish or however intense your guilt or suffering in hell, the Lord Jesus Christ will not come to your rescue. You will be cut off from the only one who is able to save you. That really will be awful.

13.
Hell's punishment

You are right. Hell is a dreadful place. And it is upsetting even to think about it. But think about it you must. Allow me to illustrate the point in a way you can easily understand.

Imagine you are ill and have to go and see the doctor. He tells you what you feared: you need surgery, and urgently too. This is unwelcome news and you are afraid. Arrangements are made for you to be examined by a surgeon and he confirms the diagnosis. There is no choice now but to accept expert medical advice. But there are questions on your mind. Is it major or minor surgery you need? What will be involved? How long will you be in hospital? Will it be successful? The surgeon answers these questions in detail and now at least you know what is in front of you.

In a similar way, you may have come to see that you are a sinner and spiritually sick before God. Perhaps through reading or hearing the Bible preached in church, you have heard the unwelcome news about hell and you are frightened. There can be no doubt about it; you have sinned and 'the wages of sin is death' (Romans 6:23). You have no choice but to accept these facts for God has revealed them in the Bible. And his Word is more reliable than the words of a surgeon.

Just like the patient, however, you want to know more about your problem and, especially, about hell. Is there more to hell than just separation? However distressing they may be, you want to know all the facts about the place.

The honest answer is 'yes'. Separation, however awful, is only one aspect of hell's sufferings for unbelievers. Another feature of hell is punishment. Yes, God actually punishes sinners in hell and he is perfectly fair in doing so. Here is information about hell which you need to know so let's think about it in more detail in this chapter.

An English minister in the seventeenth century preached on the punishment of unbelievers in hell but a group of young men in the congregation disagreed and ridiculed him for believing the doctrine. Some time after the service, one of the young men went to see the minister. 'There is a disagreement between us, sir!' the young man blurted out. 'What disagreement?' asked the minister innocently. 'Well,' the young man continued, 'you say unbelievers go to hell and I do not believe it.' The minister replied graciously but firmly, 'If that is all, there is no disagreement between us. The doctrine is taught clearly in Matthew's Gospel chapter 25 verse 46, so the disagreement is between you and the Lord Jesus Christ. Go and settle it immediately with him.'

The minister was right. He was not expressing his personal opinion nor the distinctive views of his church or denomination. Far from it. No less a person than Jesus Christ, the Son of God, taught that unbelievers will be punished in hell after they die. Listen to his words: 'They

90

will go away to eternal punishment, but the righteous to eternal life' (Matthew 25:46).

I hasten to add that the original Greek word translated 'punishment' in this verse really does mean 'punishment'. The translators have not made a mistake, as Jehovah's Witnesses and others suggest. The Watchtower translation of the word as 'cutting-off' is wrong and biased. Two examples will confirm the point. The same word is used as a verb in Acts 4:21, where we are told that the Jewish leaders tried unsuccessfully to obtain evidence by which they could lawfully punish Peter and John for preaching the resurrection of Jesus Christ. Their intention at this time was not to kill but rather deter them. The word is also used in 2 Peter 2:9 in relation to unbelievers who are being reserved in 'punishment' [1] until the final judgement. In other words, unbelievers are already being punished in this world and then in hell, but after the final judgement they will receive the full measure of their punishment. There is no doubt about it: the word our Lord uses in Matthew 25:46 means 'punishment'. In 2 Thessalonians 1:9 the apostle Paul also says that unbelievers 'will be punished . . . and shut out from the presence of the Lord . . .'

Not many people today agree with the idea of punishment. For example, we are told by the 'experts' that criminals should be treated medically and reformed rather than be punished even though they commit hideous crimes. Capital punishment for murder offences was abolished years ago in Great Britain and the use of the cane in schools prohibited. The result is that vandalism, mugging, robbery, rape, football hooliganism and inner-city violence are major problems in society.

It is no wonder then that you are surprised to learn that God punishes unbelievers in hell. You have been influenced by attitudes and standards which, although popular at the present time, disregard and contradict the Bible. In an earlier chapter we saw that God has built his law, with rewards and punishments, into the basic structure of human life and society. Now this is something which God as our Creator and Ruler has established and without which there would be anarchy throughout the world. Hell's punishment, therefore, is only the climax of a principle already operating in the world.

All right, you may reply, but what is this punishment in hell? What is involved? Is there a real hell-fire? How long will the punishment last? These are the questions we shall now consider in turn.

What is the punishment of hell? How does the Bible describe it? Our Lord tells us that the body as well as the soul of the unbeliever will be punished eventually in hell. Here is what he says: 'Do not be afraid of those who kill the body but cannot kill the soul. Rather, be afraid of the One who can destroy both soul and body in hell' (Matthew 10:28). Admittedly this will not happen until after the return of the Lord Jesus Christ to the world, but here is a reminder that even the bodies of unbelievers will be punished one day.

Conscience, too, will inflict misery on unbelievers in hell. 'It is better for you to enter life maimed than with two hands to go into hell,' our Lord says, 'where the fire never goes out' (Mark 9:43-4). Some old manuscripts add the words: 'where their worm does not die'. Either way it is a reference to a condemning conscience. You know what it means. Perhaps you told a lie recently and feel guilty about it. Or maybe you spoke some harsh words to someone or stole something that you have no right to. Your conscience won't let you forget what you did. Maybe it is something for which you can never forgive yourself. It is on your mind. Your conscience is 'nagging' and accusing you all the time and without mercy.

For some the pangs of conscience in this life are so severe and incessant that they have to be quietened by tranquillizers or drink.

In hell, however, the conscience will whip and condemn unbelievers more fiercely than ever before. There will be no peace of mind for them. One can appreciate, therefore, the Lord's description of the rich man being 'in torment' in such a dreadful place (Luke 16:23; cf. Revelation 20:10). Such torments and pangs of conscience find expression in great anguish, despair, weeping and gnashing of teeth, all of which highlight the punitive aspect of hell's sufferings for unbelievers (cf. Matthew 8:12; 13:50; Mark 9:43-48; Luke 16:23-28; Revelation 14:10; 21:8).

Is there, however, a literal 'hell-fire'? What are we to make of descriptions like 'eternal fire' (Matthew 18:8; Jude 7), 'blazing fire' (2 Thessalonians 1:8) and 'in this fire' (Luke 16:23), which all refer to hell? Clearly symbolism is being used in these expressions. Such symbolism is helpful for it lights up and illustrates the truth for us in a way which we can appreciate. But don't be fooled into thinking that this symbolism points to something innocuous and vague. Indeed, the opposite is true, namely, that the symbolism points to that which is indescribably terrible – so terrible, in fact, that it is essential to use this kind of picture-language to describe it. What, then, is the reality to which this symbolism of fire in the Bible points?

Two verses of Scripture will help us answer this question. The first verse is in Deuteronomy 4:24: 'For the Lord your God is a consuming fire, a jealous God.' A similar statement is found in Hebrews 12:29: 'For our God is a consuming fire.' These verses refer to the fire of God's anger towards sin. God it is who makes hell so terrible for unbelievers. His anger is like a fierce, never-ending fire, justly punishing unbelievers in hell without ever destroying them. Both in the realm of the body and of the soul unbelievers will suffer the fire of God's wrath without being themselves consumed, just as in a very different situation the three Hebrews in Babylon stood inside the burning furnace without being burnt in any way (Daniel 3). To answer our question, the 'fire' of hell represents the fierce anger of God upon sinners continually in hell. Be clear about this: 'It is a dreadful thing to fall into the hands of the living God' (Hebrews 10:31).

There are, however, degrees of punishment in hell. Here again is a principle we are familiar with in society. The teacher may only reprimand a pupil for talking in class but punish that same pupil severely if he cheats or steals. Similarly, an experienced athlete who, despite warning, persistently breaks the rules is likely to be disciplined more firmly than the young inexperienced athlete who ignores a rule without realizing it.

The Lord Jesus Christ applies this same principle in relation to the punishment of unbelievers in hell. Although the Lord had performed most of his miracles in the area of Capernaum during one part of his ministry, the people did not repent. He warned them: 'If the miracles that were performed in you had been performed in Sodom, it would have remained to this day. But I tell you that it will be more bearable for Sodom on the day of judgement than for you' (Matthew 11:23-24). In the preceding words he warned the people of Korazin and Bethsaida, then concluded by saying, 'It will be more bearable for Tyre and Sidon on the day of judgement than for you.'

This principle is underlined again in Luke 12 verses 47-48: 'From everyone who has been given much, much will be demanded; and from the one who has been entrusted with much, much more will be asked.' The point is clear. All unbelievers when they die will be punished in hell. There can be no dispute about that. However, those unbelievers who have a considerable knowledge of Scripture will be more responsible to God than those who have a little knowledge. Similarly, those unbelievers who sin grievously and continuously while enjoying spiritual light and privileges will be punished more severely by God in hell.

What about yourself? Are you still an unbeliever despite having Christian parents who have faithfully taught you the Bible since childhood? Or do you go regularly to a church where the Word of God is believed and taught? If so, your knowledge of the Scripture is increasing due to the church you attend or what your parents taught you.

Perhaps you do not yet go to a good church and your parents are not believers, but you have a friend or a colleague who is a real Christian. That friend tells you about the gospel of Jesus Christ and perhaps gives you some helpful Christian books to read. Appreciate all these privileges and, through them, become a real Christian yourself. But remember that your privileges make you more responsible to God when you die. If you die as an unbeliever, your punishment in hell will be greater.

In the next chapter we are going to consider the question: how long will the punishment of hell last?

1. It is interesting to notice that the verb here is in the present tense and the passive voice so we should translate the word 'are being punished'.

14.
How long?

Never before had I felt such pain and discomfort. I had just regained consciousness in hospital after undergoing major surgery. It really was agony. My tongue was parched, too, but I was not allowed even to wet my tongue with cold water. 'How long', I asked the nurse, 'will I be like this?' 'You will have to lie quietly for a couple of days,' she replied, 'but you can have a sip of water in a few hours' time.' But those few hours seemed endless to me. The nurse was right. I soon received my first sip of cold water and it was delicious. Within two days I was being moved out of bed and on the tenth day I was on my way home to convalesce. All the thirst, pain and discomfort had come to an end at last.

Another experience was possibly even more distressing and painful; that was in 1986 when I took my young teenage son to see his first rugby international match at the National Stadium in Cardiff where Wales was playing Scotland. It was a memorable game for more reasons than one! As the teams came out onto the field about ten minutes before the commencement of the game, the crowd standing immediately behind us suddenly pushed and surged forward pinning some of us to an iron fence surrounding the pitch. I shouted to a senior policeman to help us before someone was killed. He acted quickly. Several policemen and first-aid men came and lifted about thirty people, including my son, over the fence to safety and they were allowed to watch the game from the touch-line.

They wanted to lift me over the fence, too, but I was in too much pain. A couple of my ribs had been broken when I was pushed against the fence and I felt I had no choice but to refuse their kind offer. The pain was excruciating. I was oblivious of what was happening on the field. My aim was to survive by holding the crowd back from inflicting further injury. It was frightening. The time was long. Eventually the whistle was blown for half-time and I was able with some difficulty to work my way to a safer position in front of a crowd-barrier. Those first forty minutes seemed like hours and even days to me and at times I feared I would not survive. However, relief eventually came and not a minute too soon.

What is sad, however, is that there will be no end to the sufferings of unbelievers in hell. There is no prospect of their escaping or having any ease in their sufferings there. Hell is for ever and ever. And this is not my opinion but the clear teaching of the Bible.

Here, for example, is what the Lord Jesus Christ says on the subject: 'Depart from me, you who are cursed, into the *eternal* fire . . .', and a little later he says of the same people, 'They will go away into *eternal punishment* . . .' (Matthew 25:41,46). On another occasion, our Lord urges believers to resist sin even if this involves drastic action, for 'it is better for you to enter life maimed or crippled than to have two hands or two feet and be thrown into *eternal* fire' (Matthew 18:8,9). Earlier he had warned: 'Whoever blasphemes against the Holy Spirit will never be forgiven; he is guilty of an eternal sin (AV: 'condemnation', Mark 3:29). In other words, there is no prospect of the sufferings of hell coming to an end – they are eternal.

Preaching on Christ's words in Matthew 8:11-12, Charles Haddon Spurgeon – a famous English Baptist minister of the nineteenth century – underlined the eternity of hell and the fact that sinners there have nothing to look forward to except unending punishment. He says, 'They have not even the hope of dying nor the hope of being annihilated. They are for ever – for ever – for ever – lost! On every chain in hell, there is written "for ever". In the fires, there blaze out the words, *"for ever"*. Up above their heads, they read, *"for ever . . ."* Oh! If I could tell you tonight that hell would one day be burned out, and that those who were lost might be saved, there would be a jubilee in hell at the very thought of it. But it cannot be – it is *"for ever"* they are "cast into outer darkness"!'

The question arises, however, concerning the meaning of the Greek word translated 'everlasting' or 'eternal'. Does it mean 'eternal' in the sense of unending, or does it merely refer to an 'age', that is, to a more limited period? There are a growing number of evangelicals who believe the latter meaning is more correct and they are becoming more vocal in support of their theory of annihilation or extinction. In addition, these evangelicals have the support of cults like the Christadelphians and Jehovah's Witnesses. Without becoming too technical, we need to consider the question briefly.

Interestingly, the same Greek word (*aiōnios*), translated 'everlasting' in Matthew 25:46, is used many times in the New Testament and in the majority of cases it is used in the sense of 'eternal'. Think about some of these references. Both in Romans 16:26 and in 1 Timothy 1:17 the word describes the eternity of God. He is called 'the eternal God' and 'the King eternal'. There can be no doubt about the meaning of the word in these verses. God does not exist or exercise his rule for a mere 'age'. The suggestion is absurd. God is eternal in the sense that there is no end to his being or rule. Similarly, the word is used in Hebrews 9:14 where we find the phrase, 'the eternal Spirit'. Here it is applied to the Holy Spirit who, as God, is eternal. He, too, has no beginning or ending. The word is used, too, in Revelation 1:18 of the endless reign of Christ: 'I am the Living One; I was dead, and behold I am alive for *ever and ever* . . .' This does not mean an 'age' either.

Just as conclusive is the fact that the word is used over fifty times in the New Testament to describe the unending bliss of believers in heaven. As a matter of fact, the same word is used twice in Matthew 25:46, both to describe the duration of heaven ('eternal life') and hell ('eternal punishment'). Hell is eternal in the same sense in which heaven is eternal. No one suggests that heaven or eternal life is for a limited duration, so why insist that hell is only for an 'age'? Bishop J.C. Ryle summarized the biblical teaching fairly when he wrote: 'The misery of the lost, and the blessedness of the saved, are both alike for ever: let no man deceive us on this point. It is clearly revealed in Scripture: the eternity of God, and heaven, and hell, all stand on the same foundation. As surely as God is eternal, so surely is heaven an endless day without night, and hell an endless night without day.'[1]

The critics are not finished yet. In the face of this overwhelming evidence they switch their attack from the word 'eternal' to the nature of man's soul. They deny that all humans have a 'soul' which survives death. One Bible verse they misuse is 1 Timothy 6:16 where we are told of God that he 'alone is immortal . . .' 'Look', they add, 'only God is immortal in the sense that he is unending. All humans, unless they believe in Jesus, are annihilated – they do not survive in hell eternally.'

But look more closely at the words in 1 Timothy 6:16. When Paul says that God is immortal, he is saying very important things about God. First of all, he is saying God is eternal; in other words, his existence is endless. He had no beginning and he will have no end. That is true of no one else but God. Although as humans we have a soul which survives death, living eternally either in heaven or hell, yet we did not exist before our conception and birth. God alone is immortal in this profound sense of existing 'from everlasting to everlasting' (Psalm 102).

But this does not exhaust the meaning of the words in relation to God. For he is immortal, secondly, in the sense that he is the source of all spiritual life and blessedness. All the blessings of salvation which believers receive are given by God. He is the source of these privileges and happiness. Now in this double sense only God has immortality.

Is man immortal then? Yes he is, but only in so far that his existence never comes to an end; whether in heaven or in hell man will exist always. Christians, however, are immortal in a much more glorious way for they, in addition, have everlasting life through Jesus Christ (2 Timothy 1:8-12).

Now we must return to the main theme of this chapter. The punishment of unbelievers in hell will continue for ever and ever. That is the teaching of the Bible. Just as God and heaven are eternal, so hell will also be eternal.

I admit it is not easy for us to imagine the eternity of hell. One reason is that all the things we do and experience come to an end sooner or later. During the week I look forward to finishing work and returning to my family by late afternoon. Holidays are a very happy time for us as a family but they come to an end quickly. Sometimes it is a delicious meal, an absorbing TV programme, an enjoyable day out or the welcome visit of a friend or relative, and we often remark later, 'The time went too quickly.'

Yes, holidays come to an end as do examinations. A child leaves school, a young person graduates from college or completes his apprenticeship. An older person retires from work and before long his physical life comes to an end. Hell, however, is different. Unbelievers will never leave hell nor will their sufferings there come to an end. Hell really is a dreadful place.[2]

1. J.C. Ryle *Expository Thoughts on Matthew*, James Clarke, p.344.
2. For a more detailed biblical study of the subject, see the author's *The Wrath of God* published by the Evangelical Press of Wales.

15.
Purgatory and reincarnation

He is my friend and while he is only a relatively young Christian, his life is now devoted to the Lord Jesus Christ. His background is Roman Catholic but he now belongs to the Bible-believing church where he was converted a couple of years ago.

Recently he shared with me one of his concerns. 'My father died a few years ago,' he said sadly, 'and I loved him.' There was a pause and I realized he was concerned and upset. Slowly and deliberately he continued his sad story: 'Since his death, my mother pays a lot of money each year for the Roman Catholic priest to say mass and pray for my father's soul in purgatory. It is very expensive for my mother but she loved my father very much indeed. That is the reason she pays so much to the priest.'

I knew what he was going to say next. 'Now that I am a real Christian, I can see from the Bible there is no such place as purgatory. There are only two places people can go to when they die, namely, heaven or hell. Do you agree?' My answer was clear and immediate. 'Yes, you are right,' I replied, 'there is no such place as purgatory.' I asked my friend whether he knew the reasons for the Roman church believing in purgatory and as he was unsure, I explained the background to him.

'You need to understand what the Roman church teaches,' I began. 'Officially, they claim that some of their important leaders go directly to heaven when they die whereas non-Catholics or unbelievers go to hell. The majority of Catholics, they insist, go to purgatory where their sins are purged and punished. Some individual Roman Catholics may disagree with the teaching but this is the official dogma of Rome.'

My friend had lots of questions. 'How old is this belief in purgatory?' he asked. Without going into too much historical detail I explained that the dogma had been endorsed by the Council of Trent in 1546 as well as the more recent Vatican II Council in 1962-65.

'But on what evidence do they base their belief in purgatory?' he asked. He knew part of the answer and only wanted confirmation. 'Their main support for the theory', I continued, 'is a questionable statement or two in a collection of old books called the *Apocrypha,* which the Roman church added to the Bible as late as 1546 despite protests from some of its council members. These apocryphal books were not part of the Bible and are considerably inferior to the biblical books both in content and reliability.'

'O.K.,' he replied, 'which verses in the Bible, not the *Apocrypha,* do they use or misuse in order to justify their belief in purgatory?' We then looked at some of the references.

'They use 1 Corinthians 3:13 but there is no reference to purgatory here. The reference is to ministers of the gospel and their responsibility to do their work well in view of the scrutiny of their work by Christ in the Final Judgement. Another verse they refer to is 1 Peter 3:19, but again there is no support for purgatory in these words. "The disobedient" here refers to the unbelieving people in the days of Noah to whom Christ preached through Noah before the flood.'

It was almost time for us to part and go home. There were still questions my friend wanted to ask and I encouraged him to ask them.

'A priest cannot help the dead whether they are in heaven or hell. Is that right? It is too late, surely, to pray for people when they are dead.'

'That is what the Bible teaches,' I replied. 'A man's destiny is finally decided by Jesus Christ the Judge when that person dies. No amount of masses or prayers will help them after they die' (Hebrews 9:27).

He was still upset and found it hard to express his feelings. 'My mother is very sincere in her religion and she honestly thinks that she is able to help my father by paying the priest to pray for him. I am afraid she is wrong but I cannot tell her that,' he added, 'at least not yet.'

His dilemma was distressingly real. The story is repeated in many families and countries today. Only recently I read in the personal columns of a religious paper details of various Roman Catholics who died during the last ten years and for whom their families had arranged a regular mass and prayers in order to reduce their time and punishment in purgatory. Such people are sincere, of course, but sincerely wrong. There is no such place as purgatory.

To those who believe in Jesus Christ an abundant entrance is given, not into purgatory but into the everlasting kingdom of our Lord and Saviour Jesus Christ (2 Peter 1:11). On the other hand, hell, not purgatory, awaits unbelievers at death, immediately and eternally (Matthew 25:46; Luke 16:23-4). A poem written by a Welsh vicar is as relevant today as it was when first published in the eighteenth century:

> Think how death hastens, judgement comes apace,
> And heaven or hell will shortly be thy place
> (For purgatory's a mere dream, nor can
> The prayers of priests redeem a sinful man)!

Reincarnation

Just as wrong is the theory of reincarnation. A Gallup Poll in 1982 revealed that nearly one American in four believed in reincarnation, while 29% of those reading *The Times* newspaper in Great Britain as far back as 1980 also accepted this theory. Some important people have believed the theory, including former British prime minister, David Lloyd George, car manufacturer Henry Ford, composers Richard Wagner and Gustav Mahler and the German writer Goethe.

The theory has been popularized recently by a growing number of movements originating in the East or movements which have been influenced by Eastern philosophy. Yoga, for example, teaches that there will be eventual reincarnations for human beings in new human or animal bodies for as long as is necessary. Hare Krishna devotees believe that future reincarnations on earth await all those who allow passion to rule their lives here. Theosophy, a movement closely akin to Spiritism, teaches that people achieve their own salvation through numerous incarnations.

Once again the important question is not whether an Indian Guru or movement propounds the theory or whether it appeals to some people, but rather whether the Bible teaches reincarnation. We are to be guided by God's Word, not by the fallible and changing opinions of men.

The Bible leaves us in no doubt on the subject. Reincarnation is wrong. For example, Job describes death and the grave as 'the place of no return' (Job 10:21). On a previous occasion Job declared,

> 'As a cloud vanishes and is gone,
>   so he who goes down to the grave does not return.
> He will never come to his house again;
>   his place will know him no more'
>
> (Job 7:9-10).

The writer of the Epistle to the Hebrews confirms this truth: 'Just as man is destined to die *once*, and after that to face judgement . . .' (Hebrews 9:27). Our Lord's teaching consistently confirms this point.

Certainly no one can achieve his own salvation, not even through reincarnation. 'Salvation comes from the Lord' (Jonah 2:9) alone and 'it is by grace you have been saved through faith – and this not from yourselves, it is the gift of God – not by works, so that no one can boast' (Ephesians 2:8-9). One important reason advocated in favour of reincarnation is the injustice and unfairness which characterize human life on earth. This theory wrongly claims that these injustices are rectified by the purging and rewards of different reincarnations for the people concerned.

No, declares the Bible. Jesus Christ is the Judge and he will reward all men according to their works (read John 5:22,27; Romans 2:2-10; 1 Peter 1:17; Matthew 25:31, etc). All the injustices, corruption and unfairness which characterize human life and society will be judged when individuals die and then, finally, when the Lord Jesus returns gloriously to earth one day. 'God . . . has set a day when he will judge the world with justice by the man he has appointed' (Acts 17:30-31).

There is no need of reincarnation to effect justice and fair play in the world. This is the responsibility of Christ, the righteous Judge. He is judging man now and one day his judgement will be passed upon all people. Then, and only then, will there be a new heaven and a new earth, the home of righteousness (2 Peter 3:13).

Do not allow anyone to deceive you and take you away from the truth of God's Word.

16.
A warning

The nuclear plant disaster at Chernobyl, Russia, in April 1986 has been described as the worst ever disaster of its kind in the world. Quite suddenly in the early hours of the morning, the nuclear reactor overheated and caught fire, exploding and spilling out radioactive gases. These gases carry more than 10% of the radioactive waste that has built up in the fuel, amounting to ten billion curies of radioactivity.

In Great Britain the Parliament strongly criticized the Soviet Union for not informing neighbouring countries immediately of the disaster. The Swedish and Finnish governments were also angry because they were only informed of the incident after radioactive clouds from Chernobyl had reached their countries. They had not been given sufficient warning.

By contrast, God has warned people consistently over the centuries concerning the reality of sin's punishment. It was God himself who warned Adam and Eve of the punishment their sin would receive. His normal method, however, is to use men to warn people of the danger through the preaching of the Word. Noah, for example, was called to warn his people of the approaching flood. For over a hundred years God held back this disaster until the people had heard the sober warning on many occasions. They did not repent but they had been warned.

Similarly, God sent Jonah to warn the pagan city of Nineveh of impending judgement. Despite Jonah's initial unwillingness, he eventually preached the Word in Nineveh and the people repented. In this instance the warning was effective.

The responsibility of the preacher to warn people of their danger was vividly brought home to the prophet Ezekiel. Just after his call to be a prophet, Ezekiel was told by the Lord that he had been made a 'watchman . . . so hear the word I speak and give them warning from me' (Ezekiel 3:17). If Ezekiel or any other preacher does not warn the wicked that they will die for their sin then, says God, 'I will hold you accountable for his blood' (v.18).

Probably the apostle Paul had these words in mind when he told the officers of the Ephesus Church: 'I declare to you today that I am innocent of the blood of all men. For I have not hesitated to proclaim to you the whole will of God' (Acts 20:26-27). What did Paul mean? Well, remember that over a period of three years Paul had preached the gospel publicly in the city of Ephesus. But that was not all. Paul had also gone 'from house to house' (v.20) preaching the Word to families and individuals so that the Ephesians had been warned of their danger in relation to God. Paul was certainly innocent of their blood.

What about yourself? If you are already a Christian, are you warning people concerning God's punishment of sinners in hell? You have a responsibility to do this and you need to take your task seriously. Each year, over 30 million people throughout the world die. Each time the second finger of my watch moves, a person dies and goes either to heaven or hell. Do you pray to God for the conversion of these people and are you doing your utmost to reach them with this gospel? Our responsibilities are onerous indeed.

In the summer of 1986 an alert was flashed to all shipping in the English Channel after a ship carrying drums of deadly nuclear waste collided with another ship and sank about twelve miles from the Belgian coast. Governments, coastguards and seamen were all horrified at the news and the possibility of the nuclear cargo being adrift in the Channel. The maritime radio services immediately warned ships of the peril while an alert was also given to people using the beaches on the coast of the Channel. In Belgium, where the beaches were crowded for the late August holiday, thousands of bathers rushed out of the sea when the news was released.

In a more profound sense, God has issued his alert and warning to the whole world. That warning, loud and clear, is found in the Bible. The danger, of course, is far more deadly than nuclear waste; it is the prospect of unbelieving sinners suffering the dreadful punishment of their sins in hell for ever. All Christians, as well as preachers, are charged by God with the responsibility of warning people of the danger they are in.

After preaching the gospel for a few years in China, Hudson Taylor returned home to Great Britain for a brief period in order to share with churches the spiritual needs of China. One weekend during his stay in Britain he addressed a large missionary conference in Scotland. He began his talk by relating the story of a Chinese man who fell into a dangerous river in China and was allowed to drown by several onlookers. The believers in this conference were disgusted to hear of the indifference on the part of these bystanders. 'You are upset by their refusal to rescue a drowning man from physical death,' he said, 'but what of your indifference to the spiritual death and hopelessness of thousands and thousands who die each year in China without ever hearing of the Lord Jesus?' The point was well made.

Yes, all Christians have a duty to tell others about the Lord Jesus Christ. This can be done in many ways: for example, by speaking personally to relatives, friends and colleagues about their relationship to God. I was converted through a fellow-student who had promised the Lord that he would never go to bed any night without having told at least one unbeliever that day about Christ. And I was one of the unbelievers he witnessed to; after many months of faithful witness, I was converted. Are you eager to help people in this way?

Another way of helping is by inviting people to a church where they can hear the Bible being explained. Under faithful preaching of the Word, people can be converted. Do you go out of your way to invite unbelievers to your church?

Praying for unbelievers, encouraging your church pastor in his work, being involved in the life and fellowship of your local church, giving money regularly for the support of the local church and evangelism overseas – these are some of the ways in which you can help to warn people and rescue them from the awful danger of hell.

Perhaps, however, you are not yet a Christian. You have read this book with interest and you recognize your danger before a holy God. Now you want to know what you should do about it.

That was exactly the response of a prison governor in the city of Philippi in Greece nearly two thousand years ago. He asked the apostle Paul the question: 'What must I do to be saved?' You will find the words in the Bible in Acts 16:30.

This is an extremely important question because it concerns man's relationship with God. Although our relationships with our parents, children, husband, wife, brothers, sisters, etc., are very important, yet our relationship with God is much more important. After all, God created us; he is the Ruler and the Judge of all the world and, consequently, we all have a duty to obey God. This ought to be our chief purpose in living, namely, to keep his commands and enjoy him in our lives. It was for this glorious purpose we were all created. However, no man or woman does this by nature. 'There is no one righteous, not even one', declares the Bible (Romans 3:10), 'for all have sinned and fall short of the glory of God' (Romans 3:23).

Although we are all by nature sinners, not everyone recognizes his sinful condition and need. For example, the Lord Jesus referred to a Pharisee who was blind to the fact of his own sin. In fact, he was full of pride and boasted in prayer of all the good things he did. He was a sinner like anyone else, of course, but he was in the dark and wrongly thought that he was in a good relationship with God.

But do you remember the tax collector's prayer in the same narrative? (Luke 18:13) It was impossible for this man to look up to heaven because he felt his sin and guilt so deeply. 'God,' he prayed, 'have mercy on me, a sinner.' That was how the prison governor felt in Philippi. He had begun to see his own sin and though he was about to commit suicide, he knew he was not ready to meet God his Judge. That was why he asked the question: 'What must I do to be saved?' It is an important question and if you are asking this question sincerely out of a deep sense of need, there is hope for you.

Notice, too, the special circumstances in which the prison governor asked his question. Paul and Silas were prisoners in his jail and, suddenly, at midnight God opened the prison doors by means of an earthquake. Paul and his companion were now free to walk out of the prison. As the prison governor saw his prisoners walking to freedom, he decided to kill himself. Paul realized what was happening and shouted out, 'Don't harm yourself! We are all here!' The man stopped his suicide attempt and ran towards Paul and Silas. His very first words were 'What must I do to be saved?'

God works through all kinds of circumstances in order to speak to us and bring us to know his salvation. What about you? Have recent experiences or circumstances made you seek God more seriously? Are you ill? Or have you suffered bereavement or been disappointed in people? Has the experience of unemployment and its resultant hardships and trials given you more time to think about the purpose of your relationship with God? Or are you worrying about the future and afraid there will be a nuclear war? Whatever your circumstances, like that prison governor, think seriously about your relationship with God and accept your circumstances as a challenge and opportunity to come to know God.

Whoever you are, therefore, whatever your background, however sinful and ashamed you feel, there is a glorious answer to your question. Listen to the answer given by Paul and Silas to the prison governor: 'Believe in the Lord Jesus, and you will be saved . . .' They did not tell the man to get baptized, or to go to the mass, or see the priest, or do his best, in order to establish a right relationship with God. No, Jesus Christ is the only Saviour of sinners and we are saved only when we trust in him. In the next chapter we shall see how the Lord Jesus Christ saves and what it means to believe in him.

17.
A glorious rescue

It was a brilliant operation and well planned; in the annals
of rescues, it will rank as one of the most remarkable in
modern history. I am referring to the Entebbe rescue of
hostages by Israeli troops in July 1976. In case you have
forgotten the story, here are the main facts.

On 27 June 1976, seven heavily armed terrorists got past
Athens Airport security guards and boarded Air France
flight 139 that had just arrived from Tel Aviv. They took
their seats among the 246 passengers and, once the plane
was in the air, the seven operatives from Wadia Hadad
Popular Front for the Liberation of Palestine made their
move. Taking over the plane, they forced the captain to land
at Benghazi, Libya, for refuelling and then to fly the four-
hour journey to Uganda's capital, Entebbe.

At Entebbe, the terrorists released two batches of non-
Israeli passengers and kept seventy-seven Israelis as
hostages. Death was threatened for these hostages if
Palestinian prisoners in Israel and in European jails were not

released. No government was willing to concede the demands.

Israel now had no choice but to attempt a seemingly impossible rescue of the hostages. Prime Minister Rabin and Defence Minister Peres convened meetings with military chiefs. All kinds of experts and military personnel were consulted. In the end the Air Force believed they could fly as many as 1200 men plus equipment 2000 miles to Uganda, rescue all the hostages and return to Israel intact.

After some detailed rehearsals, the Israeli Government eventually authorized the rescue, using four Hercules and two Boeing 707s, one for the returning hostages and one for a flying hospital. On 4 July 1976 the rescue was completed and the hostages were walking off the Boeing at Ben Gurion Airport in Israel. The rescue raid from the skies had been successful.

Not all rescues are as dramatic as the Entebbe one. Consider, for example, the story of three young boys who watched in horror as a man hung his young dog from a tree branch by its lead and then left it to die. As soon as the man ran away, the children went to the rescue of the whimpering four-month-old mongrel dog as it dangled a couple of feet off the ground.

Or there is the case of a policeman saving the life of a young man who lay unconscious in his blazing flat. After forcing an entry into the flat, the policeman crawled on his hands and knees up a flight of stairs through intense smoke and flames to reach the young man lying unconscious in his kitchen.

Some rescue attempts, like that at Entebbe, involve injury and even death. This was also true of the pothole rescuer who fell to his death trying to save two cave divers trapped in a raging underground river 180 feet below the surface in Kingsdale Master Cave in North Yorkshire, in England. The two trapped cavers were rescued but one of the rescuers, twenty-seven-year-old David Anderson, was caught in water thundering down the cave as he was descending a thirty-foot gallery. Unable to maintain his balance, the rescuer fell and drowned in a pool at the bottom of the cave.

While these rescue stories make challenging reading, they also help us to appreciate our Lord's rescue of sinners from hell. We are going to pause for a moment to consider this.

First of all, the Lord Jesus Christ came into the world two thousand years ago on a unique rescue mission. Joseph was given a hint of this when the angel told him that his fiancée Mary was pregnant as a direct result of a miracle performed in her womb by the Holy Spirit. 'She will give birth to a son', he was further told, 'and you are to give him the name Jesus, because he will save his people from their sins' (Matthew 1:20-21). The name Jesus, therefore, describes his purpose in coming into the world.

After the Saviour's birth the angels announced the good news to a group of shepherds: 'Today in the town of David a Saviour has been born to you; he is Christ Jesus the Lord' (Luke 2:11). While our Lord taught and performed many miracles during his perfect life and ministry here, yet he entered the world primarily to be our Saviour and rescuer.

Towards the end of his earthly ministry, the Lord summed up his mission in these words: 'For the Son of Man came to seek and to save what was lost' (Luke 19:10). He was always conscious of having been sent by the Father on a special mission to save sinners.

The apostles consistently confirmed this fact in the New Testament. For example, the apostle Paul declares, 'Christ Jesus came into the world to save sinners' (1 Timothy 1:15). Just as the Israeli troops went to Entebbe to rescue Israeli hostages, or the policeman crawled through smoke and flames to rescue an unconscious man, or the young boys ran

Condemned for ever!

to rescue a dog, so, in a much more wonderful way, the Lord Jesus Christ came from heaven to earth in order to rescue sinners from the punishment of their sins in hell.

Secondly, the Lord Jesus rescues sinners from hell by bearing the punishment of their sins on the cross. Our Lord's actual rescue of his people was not glamorous nor spectacular for it involved his suffering and dying in his human nature. While he suffered in various ways throughout his earthly ministry, the climax of his sufferings came on the cross where 'Christ died for sins once for all, the righteous for the unrighteous, to bring you to God' (1 Peter 3:18).

Immediately before crucifixion, the Lord Jesus was commanded to be 'flogged' (John 19:1). For this flogging, the soldiers used a cruel torture weapon. This was a wooden handle with several pieces of rope and leather hanging from it. From these pieces of rope and leather were fixed pieces of pointed lead and sharp stones. His back bare and bent, the soldiers beat Jesus Christ many times on the back with the weapon, probably until the veins and inner organs were exposed.

It was the soldiers' turn again. In a game of 'let's pretend' in the courtyard, they collected some long, sharp spikes from a nearby shrub and pressed them down onto his head in the shape of a crown. They threw an old coat over him and marched while saluting him.

At Calvary it was even worse. Long, hard nails were hammered through his hands and feet, pinning him firmly to the two wooden beams forming a roughly made cross. The cross was then hoisted into place for all to see the victim. The people teased and laughed at him. Some even spat in his face. Others slapped him without any reserve at all. Bleeding and thirsting under the intense heat of the sun, the Lord Jesus suffered intense physical pain and discomfort.

There was, however, another dimension to his sufferings and one which we tend to forget. True, the physical sufferings and humiliation of the Lord Jesus were dreadful, but his agony became unbearable when he began to feel isolated from the Father. He expressed this deep sense of desolation on the cross in the words: 'My God, my God, why have you forsaken me?' (Matthew 27:46) They are profound words, so profound that Martin Luther exclaimed, 'God forsaken by God – who can understand it?'

William Hendriksen uses a familiar illustration to underline part of the significance of these words spoken by the Lord Jesus Christ. He pictures a young child who has to stay in hospital for medical treatment. His mother stays with him but there are occasions when she has to leave him, at least for a few minutes. On these occasions the child misses her very much and cries out for her. The point that Hendriksen stresses is that the mother still loves the child even though she is not present with her son and responding to his cry.

In a more profound sense, the Father continued to love his own Son even on the cross; Christ was not rejected at all by the Father. He had always been 'face to face with' the Father (John 1:1 literal translation) and 'at the Father's side' (John 1:18), coequal and coeternal with the Father. At his baptism and transfiguration, the Lord Jesus had heard the Father speak approvingly of him: 'You are my Son, whom I love; with you I am well pleased' (Luke 3:22; 9:35).

What happened, then, to make our Saviour feel 'forsaken' by God the Father? The Bible leaves us in no doubt regarding the answer.

'But he was pierced for our transgressions,
    he was crushed for our iniquities;
  the punishment that brought us peace was upon him,

and by his wounds we are healed. . .
And the Lord has laid on him
the iniquity of us all. . .
Yet it was the Lord's will to crush him and cause
him to suffer . .
. . . he poured out his life unto death,
and was numbered with the transgressors.
For he bore the sin of many . . .'(Isaiah 53:5-6,10,12).

'God made him who had no sin to be sin for us, so that in him we might become the righteousness of God' (2 Corinthians 5:21).

For sinners bound for hell, this is good news. The holy God we have offended and sinned against has taken the initiative in providing a substitute to suffer our punishment for us: 'God presented him as a propitiation [NIV footnote, 'as the one who would turn aside his wrath'] through faith in his blood . . .' (Romans 3:25).

When our sins were laid upon Jesus Christ on the cross, the wrath of God was unleashed upon him. The punishment we deserve to suffer was voluntarily accepted by the Lord Jesus Christ. Here lies the significance of his words, 'My God, my God why have you forsaken me?' As our substitute, the Father punished him fully for all our sins. He was not spared the wrath of God. This is why the Lord Jesus prayed in Gethsemane, 'Father, if it is possible, may this cup be taken from me . . .' (Matthew 26:39). He knew that to bear God's wrath against our sin, he would be 'forsaken' by his Father.

That is exactly what happened when our Saviour 'himself bore our sins in his body on the tree . . .' (1 Peter 2:24). Yes, it is an amazing fact. Charles Wesley, for example, felt overwhelmed when he understood the real significance of Calvary:

And can it be that I should gain
An interest in the Saviour's blood?
Died he for me, who caused his pain,
For me, who him to death pursued?
Amazing love! how can it be
That thou, my God, shouldst die for me?

There is no doubt about it. Calvary is the greatest and most wonderful rescue operation in the history of the world.

18.
Becoming a Christian

The prison governor at Philippi was left in no doubt
regarding the answer to his important question: 'Believe in
the Lord Jesus', he was told, 'and you will be saved . . .'
(Acts 16:31). This is the only God-given answer to the
question, 'What must I do to be saved?'

Jesus Christ is the only one who is able to rescue us from
hell and give us peace with God. He rescues us by his
unique and once-for-all sacrifice of himself on the cross for
our sins. 'Salvation is found in no one else', Peter declared,
'for there is no other name under heaven given to men by
which we must be saved' (Acts 4:12). The Lord Jesus Christ
confirms this exclusive claim: 'I am the way and the truth
and the life. No one comes to the Father except through me'
(John 14:6). That is why the prison governor was told,
'Believe in the Lord Jesus and you will be saved . . .' No one
else can rescue sinners from the wrath of God.

Luke records the fact that the prison governor believed
on the Lord Jesus Christ. In fact, within a few hours his

entire household had also become Christians and they were baptized with him on the following day as believers (Acts 16:32-34).

What about yourself? Where do you stand in relation to God? Are you seeking God? Do you want to become a Christian? Are you still confused as to how and when you can trust the Lord Jesus?

If so, remember that saving faith is born out of a sense of need and conviction concerning your own sin and danger before the holy God. This sense of need is often described by Jesus Christ in the Gospels as hunger or thirst. 'If anyone is thirsty, let him come to me and drink' (John 7:37; cf. 4:14; 6:35).

But the vital factor in saving faith is a personal trust in and resting upon the Lord Jesus. The prison governor was directed to trust in a person, the person of Christ, the eternal Son of God, the one who was crucified, raised from the dead and received up into glory. We must go to him in faith, rest upon him and receive him (John 1:12) as our own Saviour.

Two brief examples will illustrate this aspect of saving faith. Bishop Joseph Butler was one of the greatest defenders of the Bible in eighteenth-century England, yet in his last illness he was afraid to die. His chaplain graciously remarked to the bishop, 'You have forgotten that Christ is a Saviour.' 'True', replied the bishop with great honesty, 'but how shall I know he is a Saviour for me?' The chaplain was quick to reply: 'My lord,' he said, 'it is written, "Him that cometh to me I will in no wise cast out" ' (John 6:37). Hearing the words of Christ, the dying bishop felt a deep sense of shame and conviction. After a brief silence, Bishop Butler replied, 'Yes, I am surprised that although I have read the Bible a thousand times by now, I never felt its virtue till this moment and now I die happy.' The bishop knew about the Bible but only on his death-bed did he make a direct contact with the Lord Jesus Christ in personal faith.

The second example concerns a teenage boy. It was a cold Sunday morning in January 1850 and the drifting snow had prevented young Charles Haddon Spurgeon from going to his usual Baptist church. Instead, he turned in at the nearby Methodist church. Here the small congregation were disappointed because their minister could not reach the church because of the heavy snow. An elderly man stood in for the minister and preached briefly from Isaiah 45:22: 'Look to me, and be saved, all you ends of the earth.'

The old gentleman did his best but he was obviously not accustomed to preaching. After some brief comments on the text, he turned to Spurgeon and said, 'Young man, you look very miserable and you always will be miserable – in life and in death – if you do not obey my text. Young man, look to Jesus Christ. Look! Look! You have nothing to do but look and live!'

Spurgeon tells us what happened: 'I saw at once the way of salvation and I looked until I could have looked my eyes away . . . I came to Christ, my soul cast itself on Jesus . . . I found the Saviour.'

You are also invited to come and to believe on the Lord Jesus Christ. He will not turn you away.